THE VANISHED
LANDSCAPE

THE VANISHED
LANDSCAPE

A 1930s Childhood in the Potteries

Paul Johnson

With illustrations by the author in pen and wash

Weidenfeld & Nicolson

LONDON

First published in Great Britain in 2004
by Weidenfeld & Nicolson

© 2004 Paul Johnson

A CIP catalogue record for this book
is available from the British Library.

ISBN 0 297 84772 4

Typeset and printed in Great Britain by
Butler and Tanner Ltd,
Frome and London

Weidenfeld & Nicolson

The Orion Publishing Group Ltd
Orion House
5 Upper Saint Martin's Lane
London, WC2H 9EA

Contents

Chapter One
Smuts!

A BRIEF WINDOW opens in my memory. I am three and it is 1932. I am on top of a broad, high brick wall. How I got there is not recalled. Below me, far below, is the anxious, terrified face of my mother. Around me is the unforgettable landscape of the Old Potteries. From this wall vantage point, itself set high on a sprawling hill leading out of the city of Stoke-on-Trent, I can see the tall chimneys, belching smoke, the distant winding towers of the coal pits, above all the bottle-shaped pot-banks, each individual, each slightly different, clustered in families, around their courtyards. My mother coaxes me back to safety. 'Turn round, Paul, slowly. Now put one foot in front of the other. Slowly. Don't run. Just walk and Mummy will catch you when it is safe to jump. Slowly. Slowly. Now jump, darling, please.' Then I am in her strong, loving arms and my face is covered with kisses. She is crying with relief and I cry in sympathy. Then the window of memory closes.

The high wall, which was nearly the death of me – or so family legend claimed – belonged to a fortress-like building known as Priory House, perched on Hartshill, just outside the grimy city. It was part of a gigantic collection of ecclesiastical buildings from the third quarter of the nineteenth century, which included a church, built on Ruskinian principles, a vast convent of nuns, who managed various concerns for poor and old people, a school for girls and houses for priests. I doubt if a prior had ever lived in our house. It had been lent to my father when he first came to the district with his family to take up a job as headmaster of the Art School in nearby Burslem. The house was large, cold, damp, and my mother hated it.

Indeed, she hated everything to do with the Potteries. She and my father came from Manchester, where I had been born. Her father, and both his parents, were born there; her mother came from the Forest of Bowland, further north in the heart of the old Duchy of Lancaster, 'the fairest place on earth'. My mother was a proud Lancastrian who would willingly have fought the Wars of the Roses all over again, and who believed that savagery and chaos began at the Pennines. She was particularly proud of Manchester, to her a city of light and culture, where she had attended Sedgely College, part of the university, and where she had huge circles of relations, friends and acquaintances. Manchester rivalled Edinburgh as the Athens of the North. Its university was the best, after Oxford and Cambridge, of course. It had the Hallé Orchestra, famous all over the world. My mother had sung in the chorus of the cantata *The Mystic Trumpeter*, composed by Sir Hamilton Harty, the orchestra's distinguished conductor. Then there was the wonderful theatre, the New Gaiety, run by Miss Horniman, where all the latest plays were produced – 'before they went to London, you know' – by Sir James Barrie, John Galsworthy and George Bernard Shaw. Not that my mother approved of Shaw, as a rule. Quite the contrary, 'the worst kind of boastful Irishman and an agnostic,' but his was a useful name in her litany of Manchester delights. 'As Manchester goes, so goes the nation,' she would say and recalled for me the great struggle over free trade, which Manchester won for the benefit

Priory House and the wall from which I nearly fell, aged three

of the poor, who needed bread to be cheap. 'Always be on the side of the poor,' she said, 'like Jesus.'

Hence, to my mother the move from Manchester to the Potteries was a catastrophic descent from a high civilisation to barbarism. She had to put up with it, she said, because my father valued his new job. It was 'an opportunity to do real good' in precisely the way he chose, 'to bring art to the people'. 'Your father', she said to me, 'is a dedicated man, an idealist. Not so practical as I am, though. I have a sharper eye for difficulties and drawbacks.' I should explain that, from the earliest period of my recollection, and no doubt well before it – when I was a baby, indeed – my mother addressed to me spirited monologues to which I was not expected to reply, except perhaps to murmur 'Poor Mummy' when a particular injustice was related. It was a kind of verbal autobiography, reaching far back into the past (she was born in 1886) and embracing an enormous cast of characters, distant cousins ('once removed and he couldn't be removed far enough for me'), great-aunts, of whom there were many, known by their husbands' names, Aunt Seed, Aunt Ogilvy, Aunt Spagrass and so on; schoolteachers, benefactors, clergymen and local big-wigs like Councillor Tummage, whose speech was 'circumstantial and orotund', as my mother dismissingly put it.

Her life, childhood, schooldays, adolescence, flirtations, marriage, war and peace, work and holidays, family and friends – and enemies – were woven skilfully into a continuous and ramifying saga, brought up to date and embroidered with her present discontents, and all the setbacks and opposition 'which your poor father has to contend with'. The tone, however, was not querulous, though it could be indignant at times. It had a wonderful narrative objectivity, was beautifully clear, and spiced by quaint anecdotes and luminous metaphors. 'Aunt Seed came into the house like an admiral inspecting his flagship.' 'My cousin Aggie never missed an opportunity to leave her mark like a Pomeranian going for a walk.' 'When Aunt Sarah sat down on the open scissors, the blood fell on to the carpet like Niagara.' One of her recurrent characters was a fierce headmistress called Miss Travis, whom my mother had served as an assistant, what in those days was called a pupil teacher. 'Miss Travis did her hair in a bun and in the middle of the bun was a brooch with a bright-red glass stone, bigger than an eyeball, and it shone as if it was lit up. And Miss Travis used to say, when she turned her back on the class to write on the blackboard, "Don't think I can't see you. I have my red eye in the back of my head."'

'But was it true, Mummy?'

'It was a *strategy*. They were rough boys who needed to be

kept under control.' But another story was about how fond my
mother was of the rough boys. 'Some came from the barges
on the Manchester Ship Canal and were lucky to get any
school at all. They had no proper shoes and often only bare
feet, and they came to class without any breakfast.' My mother
would distribute pennies to the poorest, out of her minute
earnings, so they could buy a bun to eat, 'a farthing plain, a
halfpenny with currants, a penny buttered'.

My mother was horrified by the Potteries. Partly by its
poverty, for it was a low-wage area, as were all industries in
those days which employed a high percentage of women and
girls. Even so, there was much unemployment. My mother
wept at the poverty and said, 'They are so long-suffering, the
poor people. They never grumble. I have not heard many
complaints since we came here, I'll give them that.' But more
important to her than the poverty, I think, was the dirt.
'Manchester is a factory town but it is not a dirty town. It is
wet but there is no mud. The factory chimneys are tall and
puff the smoke high into the sky, and then the wind from the
Irish Sea or the Pennines carries it away. But in the Potteries
the pot-banks are so low that smoke just tumbles down into
the houses. And those horrible pot-banks are everywhere,
close up to where people live. They burn disgusting cheap
slack instead of real Wigan coal, and you can hear it exploding
in the ovens and see it jumping up the pot-banks in great
showers of sparks like nasty Japanese fireworks, and coming
down everywhere in smuts. *Smuts!*' Her voice swelled with
outrage as she pronounced the deadly word. 'In Manchester
you could not get a smut bigger than the head of a pin but
here there are half-crown smuts and smuts that would cover a
brass plaque on a doctor's surgery door. What is to be done
in a place where a beautifully washed man's shirt comes back
in the evening battle-ship grey, *or worse*? And a girl's nice new

blouse is filthy before she even gets to school, poor little thing.'

My mother's disgust with Priory House embraced its many doors, which 'let the smuts in', its mahogany surfaces, where the damp received the smuts 'with open arms' and formed an 'oily residue' impossible to dust, clean or remove without incessant effort. 'This is Smut Hall,' she said. 'Grime Grange. Pollution Palace. Find me a woman here without a smudge on her face. Or elsewhere,' she said darkly. The smudges 'come down like snow on the Russian forest'. But even worse was the particular peril of Priory House: its dark, labyrinthine cellars, guarded by a wicket gate, which I was not allowed to open, contained – cockroaches; a word my mother pronounced with histrionic dread. She told me, 'There are brazen battalions of them, lined up like Prussian infantry.' She put down borax, 'and they ate it up like high tea at Buckingham Palace' (the latter feast a Lancashire metaphor of Lucullan luxury).

I have all kinds of images of Priory House, with its horrors and dark secrets, so that as I see it today it was a Charles Addams mansion, though all the beings in it – my parents, my brother Tom, ten years older than me, my sister Clare, nine years older, and Elfride, eight years older – were precious creatures to me, loved and loving, the very opposite of monsters. My memories of it are conjured up more by my mother's saga than by my own direct experience. I never saw the cockroaches, though I imagined them in Prussian-blue uniforms dragging cannon across the cellar floors; still less the 'larger creatures' at which my mother hinted with solemn facial expressions and a finger to her lips. I had no idea what these creatures might be. Indeed, there were many passages in my mother's monologues which were incomprehensible to me, though exciting and full of resonances I retained. In talking for my delight and her own, she made no compromise to suit my tender years.

I had been born late in her life, when she was well past forty, and I had come as a great surprise to her. My nearest sister, Mary or Mamie as she was known, had died before I was born, of diabetes, then almost incurable, and all I knew of her was family folklore and a poignant photograph of her gazing with large solemn eyes at the camera from her hospital bed. My mother therefore saw me as a special gift from God in compensation for her lost little girl, and as a kind of male companion for her middle age. She treated me as an equal in many respects, or as one side of her mind, putting points for or against lines of action. So her sagas were punctuated by rhetorical questions. 'Shall we go shopping *now*, or later?' 'That man across the road, do you think he's the criminal type?' 'Do I look nice in this blue? It's Our Lady's colour you know, but perhaps, I sometimes think, not *mine*.' Later, having decided to wear it: 'I'm glad you like me in blue.'

She had an exquisite skin, pinkish and peachy, which required no make-up and certainly never received any except a dab of powder, and a trim figure shown off perfectly by her neat, unfussy, clinging garments and her brisk walk. She was graceful. Her glory was her hair, red-and-gold, which grew down to her thighs and was plaited into two thick ropes, then bound to her head by multitudes of hairpins. I watched her bind her hair every morning of my childhood, a complex operation done with great speed and efficiency, and a display of skill of which I never tired. Washing her hair was a major, emotionally fraught operation, in which I rejoiced, also conducted at virtuoso speed. She never visited a hairdresser in her life. Her sartorial maxims were magisterial: 'Silk is a material to be used with discretion.' 'No lady wears pink.' 'I love my blue eyes but I wish they were green.' 'Nothing becomes a lady more than a good tailor-made. But it must be the work of a gentleman's tailor. A dressmaker will not do.' I was confused here for I had the idea that a gentleman or knight was accompanied by a squire and wore armour. I knew my mother's corsets were a species of armour but ladies did not go into battle.

Many words used by my mother puzzled me, but also inspired imaginative images. 'Consternated' – I liked that word, which symbolised for me an angry king, for she pronounced it with grandeur. 'Loquacious' I knew had something to do with speech but I saw it as syrupy, coming out like treacle from a large mouth. She described the horrors of the cholera epidemic, still a reality in her childhood. I saw this disease as a fearsome collar, like the horses wore, only painful, hanging round the neck of the victim. 'Your Uncle Joe', she said, 'has shingles round his waist.' Shingles to me were tiny wet pebbles on a beach and I saw Uncle Joe, a fairly remote figure anyway, going around with a sparkling and shiny belt of glittering pebbles, rather like the championship belts worn by boxers – Joe Lewis and the terrifying giant Primo Carnero. 'The Mayor, if he knew, would be flabbergasted.' This was a wonderful word which I treasured, conjuring up a giant figure of rubber tyres, like the Michelin Man, suddenly deflated and shrinking as a balloon did when pricked. I was anxious to use this word. So when my mother said that Mr Swarbrick, the chemist, had fallen off his bicycle I asked, 'Was he flabbergasted?'

'No, no, no, you imp, he damaged several of his vertebrae.' I saw these things as delicate glass ornaments, perhaps connected with his shop, which he carried in his pocket.

After a time we moved into a house my father had bought and Priory House receded into oblivion, though my mother sometimes referred to its horrors. And now, at the age of four, almost five, a second window of memory opens. The attic, where I slept, overlooked the park at Tunstall, the most northerly of the Potteries towns and the nearest to the wild countryside on to which they debouched to the north and east. It looked down into the park; in fact, our address, the first thing apart from prayers I ever had to learn by heart in case I got lost, was 'Park View, Queen's Avenue, Tunstall'. In the bathroom, however — an exciting room with a giant copper cylinder to which you could cling to get warm — there was a big window which looked south into the heart of the Potteries. At night, in winter, the infernal landscape could be seen at its most exciting: flames and sparks leaping upwards out of the pot-banks, many only half a mile away, perhaps less, turning the clouds of smoke orange and pink, sometimes fiery red, the whole angry skyline seeming to heave with the frantic effort to burn and heat and scorch. I loved to watch it, this volcano nightscape, which I thought of as a natural phenomenon, not man-made. I stood on a chair, to see it better, my mother behind me. 'That is what Hell will be like,' she said solemnly, 'only worse. How lucky we are that none of us will go there, because we say our prayers.' Then she told me about purgatory which, I gathered, had smaller furnaces and less alarming outbursts of flame, and anyway did not last long. 'I hate those pot-banks,' she said. 'There must be a better way of baking the pots.' Then she would hustle me into the bath and draw the curtains, and the inflammatory nocturne would disappear.

Park View was much more to my mother's taste, though she was not slow to relate to me its numerous deficiencies, especially the old-fashioned grate in the kitchen. It 'came from Methuselah's day' and was 'from the time of the Ark'. Now I knew about the Ark and that it was made of wood. The grate was of cast iron, very much so; so this was a puzzle. Methuselah I knew nothing about and asked who he was. My mother said he was the oldest man who ever lived and his beard was longer than her hair; he was a 'phenomenon'. This was another powerful word to add to my vocabulary of mysteries. I liked that cast-iron grate and the fierce redness of the coals in it but was told it was 'more work than a bronze monument'.

Oddly enough, Mrs Williams, our maid-of-all-work, whose job it was to 'black' the grate, thought nothing of it. She was big and brawny, bold and confident, and exceedingly fond of me for she had no children of her own. She brought me handfuls of Dolly Mixtures and other contraband. She lived in what she called a 'tied cottage' (an interesting concept which gave me much food for thought) which was 'down by the tracks'. Her husband had some kind of important job (so I gathered) to do with the private railway which connected the Chatterley-Whitfield coalmine to the public line. She always referred to him as 'the Master' and I imagined him as an authoritarian giant, whose word was law. 'The Master' held strong views on many matters, faithfully reported to me by Mrs Williams. Among many things he did not 'hold with' were trade unions. Their leaders were 'a pack of troublemaking scoundrels' who 'imperilled the pit' and might cause 'a desperate accident' on the railways. They had 'taken the Kaiser's side in the war' and 'by rights should be in the Tower'. These words opened up exciting vistas. I loved the idea of the Tower where bad men went, and I repeated the word 'scoundrel' over and over again: it had a shivery ring and still does.

Replacing Methuselah's grate posed a financial problem to my mother for, though my father's position was dignified and powerful (as we shall see), his salary was not large and both my parents had a horror of debt. But my mother had a secret resource, which was of great importance to her (and me). She took in a curious weekly paper called *John Bull*. In origin it was imperialist but this was not its appeal to her. By birth and conviction she was a liberal, and a fervent admirer of Mr Gladstone and the guardian of his flame, Mr Asquith. She described the latter as 'a gentleman and that's all you need to say'. By contrast Lloyd George was 'a card turned cad'.

'Is he a scoundrel?' I asked.

'Worse.'

'Worse than a trade unionist?'

'Much worse. Trade unionists are often justified in getting fair pay and conditions.' My mother, therefore, ignored *John Bull's* politics. She bought it because of its competitions, which were many and varied. She particularly liked one called 'Bullets'. The aim here was to complete a statement with not more than four well-chosen words, expressing a true and noble sentiment, with a double meaning (not a double-entendre, of course) if possible, or a similar subtlety. The example the competition setters cited as 'the perfect bullet' was based on the clue 'For services rendered', to which the brilliant competitor had added 'King pinned on Cross', thus combining both patriotic and religious sentiments. For this a special award of £5,000 had been made.

My mother, with her love of words, was admirably suited to this game. It fascinated me too and I entered into its spirit, albeit contributing nothing of value other than earnestness, as she sat, Parker pen poised above her bottle of Royal Blue ink – the special smell of which I loved – seeking inspiration to fill in the form in front of her. She entered every week and became expert. She never won £5,000, but she had many successes: often £5, once £100 and once £500, for which sum, in those days, you could buy a new three-bedroom house. Many of her wins were in goods: a Christmas turkey, a hamper, a child's bicycle (for me), an encyclopedia and mysterious things known as 'vouchers', which could be spent in authorised places in Hanley, the shopping centre of the Potteries. I loved the vouchers because they meant she took me on a special trip to Hanley, which always included tea at Greatorex's, the principal store. Her wins were secrets between us: 'Say nothing to your father.' This was specially important when she won a fine Kodak camera, something she had always wanted to possess, but condemned by my father on aesthetic grounds: 'The camera is the mortal enemy of the artist.' He would not allow one in the house, so this precious prize had to be concealed and furtively used on particular occasions when he was not about.

My mother's 'big win', as she called it, provided the new grate, a modern, streamlined affair with all sorts of useful gadgets including a 'patent oven' — all in a pretty substance which required no blacking. Mrs Williams dismissed it as 'newfangled', but it gave my mother immense satisfaction as the fruit of her skill. It supplied, she said, 'a note of distinction' to 'an otherwise commonplace kitchen'. That word 'note' intrigued me as I had hitherto associated it with music. As such my mother, for whom music was the breath of life and its chief delight, used it often. 'Your father cannot sing a note' — and she would sigh. Or, 'I can't abide a voice which does not hit the note firmly in the middle.'

One of the pleasures of Park View, as opposed to its dark predecessor, was that she could now have a piano. She always protested that her piano playing was not 'good', merely 'adequate', rather like Anne's in *Persuasion*. She played for the public benefit when a pianist was required for singing and dancing — a role she still performed when ninety in her beloved nursing home. But she also, in private, accompanied herself and for me this became the supreme pleasure of our relationship. She would risk things in my company she was too nervous to perform for others. She loved the art songs of the great German tradition, above all Schubert, her favourite, though she always sang in English. Schumann and Mendelssohn she revered. She sang 'Lorelei', 'The Wings of a Dove', 'The Maiden', 'Night-time', 'The Swan', 'Sylvia' and Tchaikovsky's noble 'None but the lonely heart'. She loved, too, the settings of Thomas Moore's poems: 'Oft in the stilly night', 'The harp that once through Tara's halls', 'The meeting of the waters' and 'The minstrel boy', which made me, and her, cry. She knew all Shakespeare's songs: 'Come unto these yellow sands', 'Oh mistress mine' and 'Where the bee sucks'. She sang 'Cherry ripe' and 'Sweet lass of Richmond Hill'. She was not too stuffy to sing 'Daisy, Daisy' and 'Daddy wouldn't buy me a bow-wow'. She sang *The Mikado*, which she knew by heart, and *The Gondoliers*, *The Merry Widow* and *Merrie England*. She knew all the war songs, like 'If you were the only girl in the world' and 'Tipperary', and she knew the old ballads, 'Widdicombe Fair', 'Loch Lomond', 'The bonny Earl of Moray', 'Drink to me only' and 'I love a lassie'. Nobody I ever met had so much committed to heart.

She came from a time when memory training was instilled and vast quantities of knowledge were stored in the spacious chambers of the mind. She could recite all the rivers and bays of the British Isles, the principal rivers of Europe, the kings of England, with reigning dates, in chronological order, the prime ministers, from Walpole, the dominions and colonies in order of acquisition, and the decisive battles with dates. She had by heart many thousands of lines of poetry including Keats's odes, Shelley's 'Skylark' and 'West Wind', sonnets of Milton and Shakespeare, narrative poems by Southey, Hood, Tennyson and Browning — and many others — and vast chunks of Shakespeare. Even more impressive, to me anyway, was her vast knowledge of Lancashire folklore, much of which went back to medieval times or earlier, which she told with mesmerising grace and conviction. She had sayings and tales for every situation and mood, sad and gay, moral and frivolous, sentimental and fierce, often accompanied by snatches of song and verse. Her blue eyes flashed, she tossed her beautiful golden head, her hands and face mimed the emotions she conveyed, and her soft, clear voice, tuneful and full of lyric overtones — and undertones: she was a skilled whisperer of dramatic points — spoke her lines with compelling force. She was an enchantress and the countless hours I spent listening to her are rich treasures I shall carry with me to my grave.

She also, if I was fretful, took me on tours of the house, a practice she had begun when I was a baby in arms and we still lived in Manchester. In the drawing room, which contained her piano, she would show me my father's collection of etchings, by James McBey, Whistler, Nicholson and others, which decorated the walls. She would announce their titles and tell little tales about them: *Boatyard in Venice*, *A Lady at the Fountain*, *Rustic Dance*, *A Village in the Abruzzi* and so on. Then she would take me into my father's Art Room, as it was called — studio was not a term used in his circle, being deemed pretentious and un-English. There was an immense article of furniture known as the Court Cupboard, of carved, dark and highly polished oak (I think). Its high upper reaches contained doors, behind which lurked all kinds of pungent and aromatic artistic materials, the arcana of my father's profession. Down below were immense creaking doors, carved with scenes of medieval romance and ceremonial and concealing cavernous spaces in which (I noted) I could hide with ease.

An opportunity to use this hiding place occurred when my mother made an announcement. 'Your father's friend Lowry is coming from Manchester,' she said, in a voice which conveyed to me that this person was not a particular favourite of hers. 'They will want to discuss professional matters and will be in the Art Room.'

'Can I be there?'

'Certainly not. On no account are you to disturb them.' Lowry, therefore, was an artist, come to consult with my father on artistic matters. The word 'art' already had infinite and numerous associations for me. It fascinated and alarmed me, as a source – *the* source – of power and excitement. 'Your father does not approve of Lowry's work,' my mother went on, 'but he is anxious to help and encourage him. Shake hands when he comes and make your little bow, and say "Good morning Mr Lowry", then you can go.' I learned later that Lowry had been with my father at Salford School of Art but, unable to sell his work, had drifted into estate management.

The Court Cupboard in my father's Art Room in which I hid

('He is a glorified rent collector,' my mother said, which made me think that he might have golden ribbons round his neck, like a statue of the Virgin Mary.) Lowry duly arrived, a tall, lean man, as I recall, with a stick instrument of a fascinating kind I had never seen before, with a spike on the bottom end. I learned later this was a shooting stick and why Lowry carried it around with him I do not know. A symbol of office, perhaps? Or a defensive weapon, useful in the Manchester slums when collecting? While my mother was giving him coffee, I secretly slipped into the Art Room and hid myself in the Court Cupboard. I must have been four: not yet five, certainly, for school did not loom. It was dark in my arcane hole but delight stifled fear. Then my father and his friend entered. My father (I observed through a tiny crack in the door) perched himself on the high, leather-covered fender round the fireplace. Lowry opened his shooting stick and sat on it, swinging slightly from side to side. 'Well, now,' said my father, 'what I want to know is – what was it like at Old Trafford?'

'A disaster, Willy,' said the swinging man, 'a plain, unmitigated disaster.' Then followed a long discussion of a cricket match between Lancashire and Yorkshire, the notorious 'Roses' match when passions, though phlegmatic, ran high. My father, though a Manchester man, perversely always backed Yorkshire, for reasons I never discovered; but Lowry stuck to his roots, so the argument was tense. 'Painter never had a chance – a bad call.'

'Did Verity bowl well?'

'Like a cunning tiger.' Other names cropped up: 'Oldcastle', 'Leyland', 'old Bill Bowes'. The conversation shifted to other matches, other epochs. But it never left the subject of cricket. Art was not mentioned. It was the first momentous, or at least remembered, disappointment of my life. When the two left, I crept out of my lair, a cramped and disillusioned small child, baffled by the frivolity of my elders.

The Art Room was the scene of another drama of my infancy. The occasion was remarkable for many reasons. First, both my parents were away, something which had hardly ever happened (I think) since my birth. The 'elder children' had been put in charge. 'That means me,' said my sister Clare, 'for Tom is sure to slope off with his friend Marshall, on their bikes.' The phrase 'slope off' intrigued me: I saw the two boys, then sixteen or so, leaning at an angle as they vanished down the road. No matter: Clare was perfectly competent to be in charge of anything, as Elfride, a year or two younger, was a model of conscientiousness – indeed, as Clare often said, to my mystification, was 'too scrupulous'. They were two additional mothers to me, had looked after me when my mother was busy with other things ever since I could remember, and I always felt totally safe under their joint tender care.

On the Saturday afternoon (my parents were due back the next day) the girls invited their special friends, the Huntbach sisters, to tea. These three, Sheila, Doreen and Linda, went to the same school, St Dominic's. Sheila was Clare's classmate and pal, and Doreen belonged to Elfie. Linda, I suppose, was intended for me, but was two years older at least, very 'affected', I thought (to use one of my mother's words) and had a horrid doll called Andrew. This doll wore a 'monkey-jacket', which I thought boded ill. 'We shall have tea in the Art Room,' said Clare. 'Daddy won't mind.' That was presuming a great deal, but as elaborate precautions were taken to avoid spilling the least drop of tea or the smallest crumb, there was no reason why Daddy should ever know.

Then tremendous things happened in quick succession.

First it became, though only four o'clock, extremely dark. 'Tenebrous,' said Sheila, a tall, theatrical girl who was a devoted reader of Shelley. Then came a flash of lightning followed, after ten seconds — Elfride conscientiously counted — by a deep roll of thunder. Linda wailed. Doreen's lip trembled. I crept under Clare's arm. The storm was soon upon us, and the interval between flashes and thunder so short it was not worth Elfride's while to count and calculate the distance. 'We must be near the epicentre,' said Clare, already rather a specialist on anything to do with nature. 'Epicentre' was a good word, a pit presumably, but I was too tense, though not yet frightened, to savour it. This was the first storm I was conscious of, and the absence of my parents gave it further menace. It became almost pitch dark but the electricity could not be switched on, 'for fear of lightning'. Clare fetched a solitary candle and trembling fingers lit it with a Swan Vesta match from the box my father kept on his drawing table. Around this we crouched, holding hands.

'Right. Let's tell a ghost story,' said Sheila and the others felt compelled to agree, though they knew it was bravado on Sheila's part. 'Once upon a time,' said Sheila, 'there was an old house on Biddulph Moor and —'

'What was that?' asked Elfride, who had sharp ears. We listened intently, between the claps of thunder. Nothing.

Then: 'There it goes again,' said Elfride. 'It's a tapping.' We listened and I felt a quiver of fear. Linda was whimpering.

'Hark!' said Sheila. 'I hear it too. It's coming from *under the floor*.' And so it seemed to be, a gentle tapping, at intervals, but with a sinister persistence.

'Burglars!' said Clare.

'Taking advantage of the storm to break into the house,' added Sheila.

'And now they're in the cellar,' said Elfride.

'We must confront them!' said Sheila, sensing drama.

So we formed a procession, with Clare in front carrying the candle and me in the rear, holding Elfride's hand. Linda refused to come at all, to begin with; then, realising she would be left behind, by herself, tearfully joined us and took my other hand. Thus we opened the big door to the cellar and descended its dozen or so steps. The cellar smelt pungently of coal, damp and cheese, and was a most unwelcoming place, into which I had never before ventured except with my mother. It was empty. There was, however, an inner cellar, guarded by another door. 'I hear voices,' said Elfride. It was true. The thunder − the storm, indeed − had ceased. And from the inner cellar, which reached right under the Art Room, came mutterings and laughter.

'It's them,' said Clare. '*Tom and Marshall!*' She banged on the inner door and soon the two of them appeared, brushing cobwebs and dirt from their trousers.

'Oh, we had you,' they said, 'you were terrified − we heard you!'

'Not at all,' said the girls, 'we knew it wasn't ghosts. You're lucky we didn't call the police!' So the story of the Great Cellar Scare was born, and entered into family annals and mythology. I hope I have got the details right for I was very small at the time. Indeed, I have probably conflated my own vivid memories with ritualised accounts of the episode, related or changed, by my sisters on endless retellings at my request.

Tom, tall, slender, an inky but elegant fifth-former, was fond of such scary scares. He had a terrifying trick of putting a lighted electric torch into his mouth and illuminating his cheeks while putting on a 'phantom face' − this in a darkened room. He could also do a Boris Karloff limp, a Dracula posture, invoking outspread bat arms and horrid fangs made of orange peel, and a performance of the mummy rising from the tomb and unwrapping its bandages. His interest in the supernatural was intense, conflicting with his academic propensities, which were strictly scientific. He had chemistry sets galore, a real working steam engine, which he had constructed himself, a wireless set, also home-made, which received crackling messages from distant stations, a morse-code transmitter and other marvels. He subscribed to, or obtained, expert journals which assisted these projects, a source of endless fascination to me. He carried around with him and his things an aroma of 'turps' and potassium mixtures, rubber apparatus, charcoal, acids and gunpowder. He was a magus, a sorcerer, a necromancer to me.

His friend Marshall was a less potent figure, more a follower. But I was interested in his name. The family wireless, which I listened to carefully, understanding little but receiving sharp images of the people behind the disembodied voices, occasionally broadcast comments, delivered in an authoritative and almost menacing tone of certitude, by a person called Howard Marshall. His first name I understood as 'Hard' and I conceived of him as an enormous, adamantine creature, constructed of steel and granite, whose dispositions were merciless and heavy, a figure of fear. This Marshall, Tom's friend, was not like his namesake at all: on the small side, not thin but plump, morally a lightweight, so he disappointed me and I dismissed him from my pantheon. Hard Marshall, however, stayed with me for years as the voice of doom.

On this occasion the party broke up when shouts of 'Fire at Bricknall's' from the street brought us tumbling out. This was a pottery at Burslem, a mile or two away, and we could see its warehouse, struck by lightning, no doubt, blazing away merrily. Darkness was falling and the greeny-red flames of the conflagration contrasted with the orange and blue of the coal fires blasting away at other works. I became aware of the variety of fires, and their magic and beauty, for the first time, and gazed rapt until my sisters remembered the time and sent me to bed.

But this did not end the show for me. By standing on my old toy-box, a wooden cube, I could peer out of the small windows of my attic, which opened into the heart of the land of fiery furnaces, as they belched their heat and sparks and smoke into the darkening atmosphere. Thereafter it became my nightly habit to study and relish this lurid landscape, fumigerous by day, inflamed by night. My mother had opened my ears to poetry but now my eyes had perceived a strange poetry on their own.

Nor was this all. On the north side of my room another window opened on to the road, Queen's Avenue, which connected Tunstall the town with a new housing estate, just opened and immediately filled with families 'decanted' (a new term, spoken by my mother with disgust) from the terraced houses of the nineteenth-century slums. On Saturday nights the adults of this municipal dormitory, clutching the hot copper and silver of their wages — or what wives and conditions allowed — made their way on foot to the town pubs, its two cinemas and its raucous streets. Hours later, inebriate and noisy, or sullen and angry, they would tramp back. I loved to lie in my little bed, listening to their voices, excited, loving, argumentative, strident or imploring, the chorus of an old-fashioned proletariat on its night of play.

They spoke in broad Potteries dialect, a language of its own, mostly incomprehensible to me, but riveting with its thee-ing and thou-ing, its broad, urgent vowels, its mysterious sharp expletives and thrilling shouts of triumph and rage. There were disputes and fights. I occasionally caught forbidden words, like 'damned' and even 'bloody', which I knew to be the depths of wickedness, for on the only occasion I heard my father say 'damn', my mother instantly left the room. I caught a complete objurgation from an incensed virago and committed it to memory: 'Don't thou damn me, or I'll bloody well damn thee, thou – !' The last word was unknown to me and I could not grasp it even phonetically, so it became even more mysterious and important. Thus, lying in my warm bedclothes, I felt myself a silent part of a strange, intense, vibrant world, quite unlike our own, dangerous and sinister, outlawed and harsh, but curiously part of the fierce, mesmerising landscape which spewed its satanic sparks on the horizon. I fell comfortably asleep to a pandemonium.

THE GREAT ADVANTAGE of our house, as its name implied, was that it was near the park, just across the road. We had a small garden of our own and very precious it was, but Tunstall Park was my playground. I was in it every day, often (as I grew older) all day. Curiously enough, it was not my mother but my father who first took me there. Well before I was old enough to go to school he suddenly said to me, 'Little Paul, we will go to the park and I will teach you to tell the time.'

Time was important to my father. He was an enthusiast and therefore impatient. One of his favourite expressions (his pupils recalled it half a century later) was 'Do it as expeditiously as possible!' He was walking briskly, so I could barely keep up with him, and took me to the top of the park, the grander or town end, and showed me its clock tower. 'That is a noble tower,' he said, 'a significant tower.' We sat on a bench. 'The Potteries', he told me, 'are an infernal region, as your mother says, created by human greed or necessity. But their city fathers, to redeem themselves for their insult to nature, created beautiful parks. Each of the towns has its own and they are fine places a duke would be proud of. And Tunstall is the best, for it has not only formal gardens, dominated by this noble tower, but an untamed wilderness too. Now: telling the time.'

He swiftly embarked on his lesson. In those days men in positions of authority still, as a rule, carried large watches, often of considerable value and complexity, in their waistcoats, from which the chain hung in two loops. My mother's father, known as Papa to us, used to say, 'It is a mark of courtesy for a gentleman always to oblige a small boy, however dirty, who asks the time. Moreover, he must not simply *tell* him the time, even if he knows it: but *show* him, for that is the bit a boy likes.' In his case this meant slowly pulling on the gold chain until the watch emerged, like a jewelled monster from its cave. Then he pressed a hidden spring and the gold case of the watch magically opened. The next move was to touch the repeater, which quietly chimed the hour. Finally the minute and second hands were consulted, shown to the boy and the exact time solemnly pronounced. Papa concluded, 'And that's what it is o'clock, my boy, unless Greenwich Mean Time itself is wrong.'

My father had a wristwatch – 'It's quicker' – so chose to teach me how to chronomicate, as he put it, by the park clock, which also involved a lesson in architecture and in distinguishing between Arabic numerals, as on his watch face, and the clock's Romans. All three matters became delightfully confused in my mind. To be alone with my father was a privilege, rarely granted, for he was busy – running his school, pursuing his own career as an artist, doing countless voluntary tasks his conscience and enthusiasms imposed. His life was a hectic, uninterrupted voyage between duties. Unlike my mother, whose teachings were essentially personal and often had an intimate autobiographical angle, my father expounded great sweeps of information about the objective world. He had huge stores of arcane and specialist knowledge, as well as academic lore. He was dark – he claimed 'proud drops of Spanish blood' – balding, not above middle height, but well made and strong. He had a fine Roman nose, not originally but as a result of 'a disputation with the Albert Memorial in a dense fog' (this was the Manchester version, opposite the Town Hall). He was an orphan, whose parents had been wiped out in the first big influenza epidemic of the 1880s. He had not liked his stepmother, who had tried to make him eat a boiled egg he pronounced bad – he was a perfectionist. As a result, he had run away to sea at the age of twelve, which was perfectly lawful in those days. He argued that his Spanish blood sprang from the Armada of 1588, many of whose ships had been wrecked off the western coasts and the survivors denized (his term). So sailing was his heritage.

On this, or perhaps on another occasion, he told me the story of his first voyage, on a four-masted sailing ship carrying 'piece goods' across the Atlantic, from Liverpool to New York. The Master, Captain Matthews, was kind to him and began to teach him navigation. When they docked at New York 'near the Battery', the Master said, 'You may go ashore, Boy Johnson, but just to look. I am giving you none of your pay so you get into no mischief.' So my father disembarked and wandered around the waterfront of that great city, just beginning to shoot up its skyscrapers.

Eventually, feeling hungry, he spotted a blackboard outside a bar which read 'Free Lunch'. My father never lacked courage, or enterprise. He had a bold streak. So he entered, climbed up a tall bar stool and announced, 'Free lunch, if you please.' The barman – big, jovial, in a long white apron – handed him a fine plate of steaming corned beef hash. 'No such food has ever been served to a hungry boy,' said my father. 'It was nectar.' (Perhaps this explains why corned beef hash has always been my favourite Yankee breakfast dish, since I first sampled it in 1955.)

Then the barman said, 'And what'll it be to drink, laddie?'

My father replied, 'Oh, nothing. In the first place I don't drink. And in the second I have no money. But the hash is delicious.'

The barman put his hands on his hips and said, 'Waal, I'll be daamed.'

My father explained that the public parks were designed to give humble townspeople the feeling they had free access to property not unlike the parks of the highest aristocracy, 'such as the Duke of Sutherland at Trentham'. Tunstall clock tower was the centre of a formal garden which gradually led to serpentine paths, temples, follies and grottoes. All this part was enclosed, like a fortress, by a terrace built on a rusticated stone wall, with the rest of the park twenty feet below. I loved this arrangement, constructed with ingenuity and a sense of monumental grandeur. Below it was a parade ground, for ceremonial occasions, flanked by bowling greens of velvety turf and tennis courts of bright brown ash. And beyond were the lakes and the wilderness.

My normal custodian in the park before I was old enough to go there by myself was my sister Clare, usually attended by Elfride. I loved Clare with the same mixture of passion and admiration I felt for my mother. Clare was a kind of natural divinity, a goddess of the wild. She could do anything: run fast, jump high and far, hurl a cricket ball vast distances, swing a tennis racket with dazzling strength, whistle better than most boys and climb trees like a squirrel. She knew the names of all trees, most flowers, could recognise leaves, identify the provenance of pebbles, having a collection of the rarer varieties, and in season collected the hardest conkers ever known in the district. She distinguished between all the common birds and, by intense observation, knew what they were doing. Animals loved her. Dogs came up to be petted, even fierce ones; cats rubbed and purred, birds pecked tiny

Tunstall Park from our house

pieces of bread from her lips. She noticed everything and her eyes were often on the ground searching. She found innumerable four-leaf clovers and once a five-leafer, plus many minute wildflowers she collected and placed amid nests of moss and exquisite small stones and shells. In her searches she often came across the tiny silver threepenny bits, one of the delights of those days, which fuddled potters had let slip on their Saturday night trudges home; sometimes a sixpence — wealth to us.

Clare looked after our pets. We had a series of canaries, always called Dick. (Budgerigars were thought vulgar.) If we had a tortoise it was called Bob. We had a tame hedgehog, too, called Sheridan, but it went mad and ran round endlessly in circles, to Clare's tearful distress, shocking to me because she made a point of never crying. She kept close watch over the neighbourhood, its animals, trees and flowers. She was the heroine of the one example of crime that occurred in all my childhood. She noticed that a ten-foot birch tree, newly planted by the council near our house, had been malevolently stripped of its bark by 'wicked boys'. The missing portion was four inches deep all round, sufficient in Clare's opinion to kill the young tree. So she got from our friend, Dr Halpin, a stout bandage, and bound it round the tree over and over, until it was warm and protected. Meanwhile, she had alerted the police, in the shape of Detective Constable Fenton, who lived not far away and who, having inspected the tree, pronounced it 'a clear case of vandalism' and commended Clare for her vigilance. The tree survived, the wicked boys, or at any rate some wicked boys, were apprehended and the case was closed.

Clare was the heroine of another drama involving me. When I was small she combined taking me to the park with doing shopping for my mother, using for this purpose a pushchair I had really outgrown, which kept me penned while she was busy in the shops and had a capacious basket at the rear. She liked to feed the fowl in the upper of the two lakes in the park. Ducks were at home in both but the swans would not frequent the lower, larger lake. Clare said, 'Swans are choosy birds.' On this occasion she had finished her shopping, safely stowed behind me, and was dividing a piece of stale bread into portions for her swans, which she knew by name and character. I was parked some distance from the lake, which had a sloping rim. Her voice came to me: 'No, Ariel, you've had your share already. Don't be greedy. Let Beatrice have a turn. Now, Talisman, here's a piece for you. Don't snatch – you nearly bit me. Be a graceful swan! Artemis, catch!' I was restless, penned in my chair. And curious, for the lakes were connected by a dark tunnel half full of the water that flowed from the upper to the lower basin. It was a place of terror for me, for I could imagine myself entering the tunnel, getting stuck, then suffocating or drowning. But I wanted to see its evil mouth more clearly. So, I recall, I stretched out a foot from my pushchair, touched ground and propelled it forward a little closer to the lake; then another. To my consternation (my first opportunity to use this powerful word of my mother's), the pushchair gathered momentum, for it was now on the slope, and in a few seconds it, and me, shopping and all, were in the lake.

My window of memory revealed exactly how I got into the water but not what happened afterwards. At that point family legend takes over. The pushchair hurtled deep into the lake, scattering the shopping, so that plums and potatoes and apples were soon bobbing in the water to the delight of the swans, and I was trapped beneath the waves. But Clare plunged in and, being a strong swimmer, pulled me and the pushchair out, watched by a collection of goggling old men, alerted by the drama. She was pronounced 'a grand girl' and myself 'a brave boy' not to be crying. The park superintendent was notified and hurried over, to see if any rule had been broken. But, taking in the scene, he praised Clare for her prompt rescue bid and arranged to have 'the Park vehicle', a van, take us swiftly home, pushchair included, 'before you get your deaths of colt'. Clare was alarmed at the prospect of my mother's rebuke for losing the shopping. Instead, she found herself hugged and fussed over almost as warmly as I was, and many tears, of relief not anger, and thanks to Divine Providence, marked our saturated homecoming. I believe the episode even merited a paragraph in the *North Staffordshire Sentinel*. It certainly won the commendation of Miss King, the all-powerful gym mistress at St Dominic's High School for Girls. Clare was already her favourite, on account of running and jumping – she went on to win six silver cups and trophies

— but here was a splendid opportunity for Miss King to demonstrate how vital it was that 'every girl must learn to swim'. So Clare stood high in the esteem of all and I basked in her reflected glory.

This incident put my sisters in mind of the fact that I could not swim. Elfride could and, though she did not yet know the crawl, which Clare performed with powerful efficiency, she could do breaststroke and backstroke, and even dive. I could do no more than dog paddle and it was clear a vigorous series of visits to the town swimming bath was needed. But how? Under municipal regulations there were 'Ladies' Days' and 'Gentlemen's Days'. 'Mixed' swimming days were rare, only on certain Saturdays as a rule, and were 'pandemonium' as my mother said, impossibly crowded with 'rough boys', who could be counted upon to be 'dirty' and display 'offensive habits'. Therefore they were forbidden. The municipal mind did not encompass means to allow girls to teach their younger brothers to swim.

Hence Polly was born. My sisters often dressed me up in girls' clothes for purposes of theatricals they devised, in which boys rarely featured. I was used to playing non-speaking parts, garbed as 'a lady of quality', a parlourmaid, a 'cottage woman', a flapper (a term still in vogue for some years after the flappers got their votes in the 1929 election) and even as a princess, with a one-line part: 'You may rise, good people.' I had worn skirts, nighties and pantaloons. Moreover, it must be remembered that in my mother's time it had still been common for boy children to be dressed as girls until aged three or more, when they were formally 'breeched'. So it was not such an astonishing idea to garb me as a little girl to circumvent municipal rules against mixed bathing. Needless to say, the ruse was determined by Clare, always opposed to rules she felt were 'against nature'. Elfride, strict in her observation of all regulations, parental or scholastic, was apprehensive about taking me through the streets disguised and slipping me through the turnstile at the Tunstall Public Baths under the fierce eye of the Assistant Baths Mistress, Mrs Scurridge.

But Clare's certitude and determination carried her along, as they usually did. A small dress, long discarded, was found, stockings, a beret, sandals, even a coral necklace. My bathing suit was, anyway, unisex (not a word then used). I had a towel with the initial 'P' sewn on it in red. 'What shall we call him?' asked Clare.

'Polly,' said Elfride.

'Excellent! Polly it is!' As I was already referred to, often, as Ponka or Ponker, Paulie, Paulie-Waulie and 'Poor Paulie-Waulie', this was no great burden to be borne. My mother, apprised of the plan, secretly approved — she, like Clare, was an antinomian by instinct — but her official line was 'I know nothing about it'.

So the three of us set off and Clare, even Elfride, enjoyed it hugely. They loved calling me Polly in the hearing of others, so it was 'Polly put your beret on' and 'Polly don't drag your feet' and 'Polly *come on!*' all the afternoon. My long, brilliantly red-gold curls could easily have belonged to a girl anyway. But they were conspicuous. We got through the turnstile with no trouble and I changed in Clare's cubicle. My swimming lesson proceeded without difficulty in a half-empty pool. But a nosy little neighbour called Cynthia Chapell, with whom we were not encouraged to play because her father was 'a leading Freemason and not just for show either', as my mother put it, spotted the fact that I was there on Ladies' Day. 'What are *you* doing here, with your horrid carrot-top head? You will certainly be sent to prison for breaking the law!' — which made me cry.

But Clare came to the rescue, tearing through the water

with flashing strokes like Johnny Weissmuller playing Tarzan, and drew me swiftly out of Cynthia's orbit. Moreover, she launched a devastating counter-attack on the horrid girl: 'Don't you know you're not allowed a rubber lifebelt in the shallow end?' she ad libbed resourcefully. 'Or to wear swimming shoes on a weekday? I'll have to tell Mrs Scurridge, I fear.' So that made Cynthia cry and we heard no more of her. We returned home triumphant. But I was not anxious to repeat the deception, having conceived a dislike to being Pollied. Shortly after, 'Juvenile Mixed Bathing' became a municipal fact of life and I learned to swim legally. But the tale joined the family saga and I was sometimes Pollied again, not just by my sisters either.

My sisters took me to the park every Saturday and every day in their school holidays. There was a little iron gate in the railings almost opposite our house, which was opened at eight in the morning and shut at dusk, and this led straight into the wilderness. On a weekday we usually had it all to ourselves. We played games, often of a fantastic nature, worked out by my sister Elfride, already a 'bookworm' as my mother said. Clare studied the trees and taught me to climb them, though it was supposedly forbidden. Park keepers were strict in those days, real authority figures: often former NCOs from the guards, who had 'been in the trenches'. They had stubby, bristling little moustaches, which looked, said my mother, 'as if they had been hammered into their faces from the inside', a gruesome concept I took literally. But they never came near the wilderness, where there was nothing to spoil. We took with us a basket with a bottle of water, and into the water, when we were thirsty, we inserted little lozenges, which turned it into a species of lemonade, orangeade or ginger beer, depending on the colour of the lozenge, yellow, orange or white. It fizzed and was palatable. Sometimes we had fruit in season, especially plums, which were a penny a pound, or even given away free at garages and some shops, in return for a purchase.

Sweets were normally eaten only on Saturday morning, after we got our pocket money. I began with a halfpenny when I was five, gradually rising by a halfpenny a year. The others got more — how much I don't know. We got our sweets at Mrs Keely's in King William Street. My mother described her as 'an unclean woman', which she certainly was and might well have been a witch in earlier times. She was surly, bad tempered and smelt powerfully — of spirits no doubt and other things. She swore when provoked by 'wicked boys'. On the other hand her sweets were cheaper than anywhere else, she sold them in minute quantities, wrapping up a farthing's worth in a paper scroll, and her portions were generous.

The range was wide: acid drops, pear drops, Mint Imperials, aniseed balls, bull's-eyes, lavender lozenges, banana glories, gobstoppers, raspberry shapes — all sucking sweets, guaranteed to last longest. There were Pontefract Cakes, liquorice allsorts and dolly mixtures, bootlaces and girdles, also liquorice, Brazils (expensive and not recommended), honey nuts, coconut ice (for long my favourite), walnut chocs and sugared almonds, marzipan marvels, Broken Chunks (cheap but of inferior chocolate), various caramels, wrapped and un-wrapped, Treacle Sweets (wrapped), treacle toffee, in slabs broken by a silver hammer, and various other jaw breakers. Brands like Quality Street, let alone Cadbury's Roses, were too expensive, as were all boxed chocolates like Milk Tray or Black Magic, then new. But there were halfpenny wrapped chocolate bars from Fry's and a penny Turkish Delight. I remember the first Mars Bar 'coming in' and the following year the answer to it from a rival, Milky Way. These cost a penny. One year a new kind of white chocolate appeared,

which you bought in 'portions', but unwrapped. Elfride loved
the idea as she loved everything white, being 'pure'. But when
she got hers home she discovered on the virgin chocolate the
unmistakable marks of Mrs Keely's fingerprints and tearfully
pronounced it uneatable. 'Tosh and rubbish!' said Clare
cheerfully, seizing the chocolate and putting it under the tap.
'If you won't eat it, I will!'

Words like 'tosh' crept into the girls' vocabulary from their
readings of school stories. There are some strange gaps in my
knowledge of children's literature due, I think, to objections
raised to texts by one or other of my parents, who held strong
views on suitability. Thus *The Pilgrim's Progress* was vetoed on
religious grounds no doubt; why *The Wind in the Willows* was not
approved of I do not know, for my father greatly admired the
illustrator Arthur Rackham and positively worshipped Sir
John Tenniel, who helped Lewis Carroll to bring *Alice in
Wonderland* to life — but this too I never read.

My father was interested in Anglo-Saxon and medieval times,
hence Elfride's name and my second name, Bede. My mother
had a story that he had wanted to call Elfride Frideswide and
me Egfrith, but that, I think, was glorious hyperbole. He
presented me, before I could read, with a delightful book on
King Alfred, with superb illustrations of Saxons fighting
Danish invaders — including one of a thegn being relentlessly
pushed into a pit full of hissing snakes, an image which stayed
in my mind. The first book I read through, under his guidance,
was a simplified edition of Froissart's *Chronicles*, with good
pictures, including a startling one of the naval battle of Sluys,
which I copied many times. There was also a child's *Idylls of the
King*, with the marvellous image of the arm reaching out of
the mere to receive Arthur's sword. My mother read me the
key verses, over and over.

But if I missed some children's classics, I enjoyed other books that do not normally come the way of boys. Clare amassed a large collection of school stories beginning with Angela Brazil. One reason Brazil was approved by authority was that each of her stories was set in a different location, allowing the author surreptitiously to impart geographical and historical information to her readers. Clare thought her 'a bit goody-goody', but allowed she told 'fine yarns'. The story set in Naples had a fascinating (illustrated) episode in which a fourteen-year-old girl hid in a giant Italian garden vase. This intrigued me but I looked in vain for such a thing in my neighbourhood. My father, questioned, said, 'Wedgwood's made an even bigger vase for Queen Victoria but small boys are certainly not allowed anywhere near it.' So that was that.

Brazil was succeeded as favourite by books written by Dorita Fairlie-Bruce, about a bouncy girl called Dimsie – *Dimsie at School, Dimsie Moves Up, Dimsie in the Sixth* and so on. Then came Elinor Brent-Dyer's arresting series, beginning with *The School at the Chalet,* about an orphaned family of girls who set up a school in the Austrian Tyrol near a TB sanatorium. There were elaborate descriptions of Austrian pastries and how good Austrian coffee was (with cream), and an underlying theme of the books was that the nicer girls, when they matured, married handsome doctors from the 'san'. It has since struck me that my reading of these stories, and discussing them with my sisters, gave me imperceptibly a useful insight into the female mind, and helps to explain why I like women so much and have such warm friendships with them.

Anyway, on fine days we took books into the park and read them there, often aloud. When Clare discovered Arthur Ransome's stories about the Lake District, we tried to re-enact episodes in the wilderness, imagining it to be Westmorland scenery, and took boats out on the lower lake, imagining they had sails. The girls loved *Swallows and Amazons* so much that they bought it second-hand; and when *Swallowdale* came out, not having enough cash, they borrowed the Tunstall library copy and transcribed the entire text, taking turns, in school exercise books. This almost incredible labour, or so it seems to me now, was accomplished in a fortnight, at the end of which the book had to be returned, and involved midnight sessions, unknown to my parents. Then the text was available for repeated readings and large sections were learned by heart. The effort reflected the passion and dedication my sisters brought to books they loved, which they imparted to me.

Elfride did most of the writing. Her hand was small, neat, legible and elegant – Clare's more careless, as befitted a poet, for it was about this time she began her Scandinavian-type epic poem, *Finn*, a grand saga, never finished but never relinquished, about a Norse sea adventurer. Elfride wrote poetry too, but she was more interested in the craft and actual activity of writing than Clare was. Where Clare collected leaves, dried flowers, clovers, pebbles, rare pieces of bark, fossils and insects, Elfride liked pencils, meticulously sharpened, clean rubbers, pens, inks, notebooks and writing paper of all descriptions – the elements of a modern scriptorium. Desks were important to her. So were envelopes, letters, postcards and any post office impedimenta such as rubber stamps. She liked the smell of these things when new and so do I. She adored neatness, order, long columns with perfectly aligned left-hand margins and developed a rare skill of writing whole pages on plain paper without having to rule lines in pencil first.

Both she and Clare loved to do diagrams in pencil, putting in all the names in ink – for botany, geography, maths and any other purpose. They taught me how to do likewise.

Indeed, they taught me everything, during long sessions in the park, in the spring sunshine and the *longueurs* of summer afternoons. History and geography came first. Elfride taught me history methodically, reign by reign, culminating in the glorious eighteenth century, when the Empire expanded over the world. Blenheim, Plassey, Quebec, the Battle of the Saints were familiar names to me, Blake and Clive, Marlborough and Pitt the Elder early heroes.

Clare's lessons, about nature, were less systematic, more intense. She would suddenly begin a passionate disquisition on clouds, or the variety of ferns, or geological layers. She loved dinosaurs many decades before they became fashionable. So tyrannosaurus rex and pterodactyls peopled my infancy, along with Georgian soldiers and admirals. My sisters shared with me their delight at learning new things at school. Just as my mother accustomed me to big words and strange expressions, Clare and Elfride filled me up with every kind of information that struck them as important. They taught me verses by heart, and I learned Latin conjugates and declensions before I could read English; even a little Greek. They read me, too, Charles and Mary Lamb's *Tales from Shakespeare*, that magic casement opening into the wild wide sea of the greatest of all writers.

There came a day when I was old enough to go into the park by myself. The reader must forgive me if I skip back and forth a little in time, following the logic of place and topic rather than strict chronology. It amazes me now, looking back, how free my life as a small boy was, how little I was supervised and how confident my parents were that I would come to no harm. Children today, by comparison, are prisoners of the evil which walks in the world. I was never molested. Nor did I know, or hear of, any child who was. Crime played no part in our lives. No door was ever locked except when we went on holiday. I never was told of any theft. If you dropped something in the street the person who found it would go to considerable trouble to find out where you lived and return it. Poverty was everywhere but so were the Ten Commandments. God saw everything you did, or did not do. All stories, books, plays, films, comics – I am tempted to add newspaper articles – had a moral purpose, implicit or open. No child I knew would have dreamed of trying to shoplift, let alone boast about it, as children now are said to do. The punishment would have been draconian, moral as well as physical, and affecting all the family. The prison population was only about five per cent of what it is now. If anyone had been to prison his family took desperate measures to keep it quiet. My mother spoke of such things in whispers, as though they occurred in a distant land.

Nevertheless, she liked me to go into the park with 'a friend'. That friend, in the first instance, was Teddy Stone, my age, who lived in our street. He was strong, patient, equable, easily bidden as a rule, good-tempered and monumentally dull. His mind worked slowly, like a shunting engine, travelling along predestined lines to inevitable conclusions, which could be guessed long before he got there. He was also clumsy. Toys came to pieces in his hands. Buttons, laces, ties, collars baffled him. This was curious, for clothes played a starring role in the economy of the Stone household. Mr Stone, a rather silent, withdrawn man, chiefly notable for a set of miniature war medals Teddy proudly showed me, had some managerial post and they were certainly not poor. There was indeed talk of the Stones 'buying a motor', though nothing came of it. But at birthdays, even Christmas, their boys, Teddy and his elder brother Fred, a lugubrious, tall teenager, were given clothes rather than proper presents. My mother thought this outrageous. 'What did you get for your birthday, Teddy?'

Teddy, echoing his mother: 'A splendid pair of brand-new boots.' Fred got 'a first-class Burberry raincoat'. 'Presents' included socks and shirts, sets of studs, braces and even toothbrushes.

That was the way Mrs Stone's mind worked. My mother said nothing about her, but to me, instantly responsive to the slightest inflection of her opinions, it was clear my mother despised her neighbour. I did not like her either, for a variety of reasons, and tried my best to avoid setting foot in their house or even their backyard and garden. In the first place Mrs Stone (whose name was Laetitia, never used by anyone: Mr Stone, on the very rare occasions when he addressed her, called her Letty, which made my sisters giggle uncontrollably) had a dog called Boy, a foul-tempered creature who emitted hostile noises at all times and appeared ready to bite anyone except his mistress. His horrid nose screwed itself up into what I called a 'snowl', a word I had unconsciously invented, to my mother's delight. But Boy was no joke to me. I feared him, especially since Mrs Stone did nothing to curb his hostility. 'He doesn't seem to like you, Paul,' she said triumphantly. 'I wonder why?' – as though this unlovable creature was a sure judge of bad character. He bit Teddy too, although that was pronounced to be 'in play'. But Boy was not at all a playful dog, or if he was, he always played for keeps.

Mrs Stone was deeply suspicious of my relationship with Teddy. He was older than I by six months but she judged me a bad influence, certain to get 'poor Teddy' into 'trouble' or even 'bad habits'. Of course, it often happened that I had to take the lead, since Teddy had no strong inclinations of his own. He had certain gifts. He could whistle powerfully. He could make a loud popping noise with his finger in his mouth.

He had a repertory of couthless noises, in fact, including dismal snarls, made when we were fighting with our toy soldiers. These battle-cries were variations of 'Drrr-drrr-yoowole-dsyssss-drrryowllyowl', accompanied by expectoration and heavy breathing. Teddy delighted in these noises and I had no objection but my mother, hearing them, pronounced them to be 'reprehensible' and 'disgusting'. Moreover, Mrs Stone did not like them either, since in her next litany of complaints that she delivered about my bad influence on Teddy was a new item: teaching Teddy 'common noises' – common meaning, in this context, uncommon and vulgar. This accusation left me speechless and baffled. Teddy said nothing either, as he had learned to turn a deaf ear to his mother's litanies. He accepted her as a fact of life about which he could do nothing. Indeed, I never heard him refer to her at all.

Teddy and I got on perfectly well. He got into trouble, occasionally, through thoughtlessness. There was no malice or wickedness in him. But he was indeed clumsy. He tore his clothes. He attracted mud. He scraped his knees. (Boys always wore short trousers, then, and long socks.) Once he got a black eye falling off a see-saw. I was blamed by Mrs Stone for these mishaps. She hinted his black eye was my doing. For once Teddy broke his silence. 'See-saw, Mum, I told you. Paul and I never fight. There's no point.' I dreaded Mrs Stone's sermons.

Indeed, there was only one reason I ever set foot in their house. Though it was not decorated with paintings, drawings and etchings, as ours was, it did possess, hanging over the kitchen fire, an extraordinary print or steel engraving. It was called *Vanity Fair* and showed a procession of worldlings, led by a tall, fashionable woman, scantily clad in an outré evening dress, descending a staircase. The picture was full of incident and wicked characters, devils too. I loved it. It compensated for Boy's snowls and 'Letty's' harangues. Was this minatory picture her choice or Mr Stone's? The house and life bore no suggestion of vanity or exotic behaviour – quite the contrary. Mrs Stone's appearance was unmemorable. In fact, I always averted my gaze as she addressed me with complaints, no doubt an admission of guilt to her. She called me 'hangdog', a word I found puzzling. Were dogs hanged? If so, what about Boy?

Then came 'the accident'. One morning, soon after eight (it was the holidays), Teddy and I sought out the iron gate in the railings that protected the wilderness from unauthorised entry. It should have been open by then, but it was not. I said, 'We'll come back later.'

But Teddy had a kite, an unexpected present from one of his father's customers, and was anxious to fly it while the wind was strong. He said, 'We can climb over.'

Now this struck me as difficult and dangerous, for the rails were about five feet high and terminated in spikes. I flatly refused and told him not to attempt it. 'What'll your mother say if she hears?' I asked.

To which he replied, to my surprise, 'She be damned!' – a dreadful remark that shocked me deeply, which Teddy must have picked up from his brother, or possibly his father. He then scrambled up the rails, got to the top for an instant, slipped in his brand-new splendid boots and fell. A spike went straight through the fleshy part of his right hand and, thus crucified, he hung there with a puzzled expression on his face, leaning against the rails. He never said a word or uttered a cry but began to lift his hand off the spike. I helped him and we got it off, which must have been extremely painful. But he made no complaint, though the blood flowed and some fell on the kite. I hurried him home, leaving a trail of blood spots, holding aloft his injured arm in one hand, clutching the kite in the other.

We met no one, except an old man who said, 'Ee, lad, thou art in reet trouble, dost thou know? What wilt tha Ma say?' That was exactly the thought that filled my mind too.

Our entry was dramatic. Mrs Stone screamed. Boy cowered. Fred commented, 'That's sure to go septic. They may have to cut your arm off, Teddy.' Then the vials of Mrs Stone's wrath poured upon me, culminating in 'Look at the kite! Covered in blood!' Teddy said nothing, then or later. Dr Halpin, summoned, said the wound was 'mercifully superficial' and gradually things calmed down.

My mother's comment was, 'Why does she make him wear those dreadful boots? It would never have happened if he wore pumps like other boys.' I never saw *Vanity Fair* again.

I HAVE NOT yet mentioned the building that dominated our lives as well as our neighbourhood: the Catholic church. It was enormous and it was near. Indeed, only two houses separated us from it. The first belonged to the Handles, a wealthy family who owned shares in a successful pot-bank and other concerns. Mrs Handle was, I think, sofa-bound and we hardly ever saw her, except the rare glimpse of a fur-wrapped figure stepping into her motor. Mr Handle was portly, ceremonious and smoked a cigar. They had one child, a little girl called Geraldine. If she had friends, she had to be driven to see them, for she did not mix with the local children. In any case I was not allowed to play with her as Mr Handle, too, was a Mason, indeed a 'Big Mason' (another puzzle as he was, if anything, short in height). My mother said his wife was 'difficult' and 'a case', so I saw her as a sort of walking coffin. Geraldine stuck out her tongue at me, something I had always been strictly forbidden to do, so I dismissed her as badly brought up. When I became attached to the *William* books, I saw her as Violet Elizabeth Bott, who constantly threatened to 'thcream and thcream till I'm thick'.

On the other side of the Handles was the presbytery and beyond that the church itself. As it was the first church of which I became conscious, as well as our own, it became the archetype and epitome of all churches to me, and the standard of comparison for other churches. Once I was old enough to nip out by myself, I was in and out of it all day and every day. It was a sacred playground to me. I took its grandeur and enormity for granted, even though my mother called it a 'phenomenon' and an 'extravagance'. But the truth is it was and to this day remains a most unusual church. My father would look at it and sigh deeply. It was a worry and a burden to him and, I think, pained his deepest aesthetic sensibilities. But he would never say a public word against it: he had seen too many shattered medieval churches in Flanders, during the four years he spent at the Front, to complain against a vast new church. He quoted Job: 'The Lord giveth us churches and the Lord taketh them away. Blessed be the name of the Lord.'

The church was the work of one man: Father Patrick Joseph Ryan, parish priest of Tunstall, 1903–51. He had been in this benefice for thirty years when we first moved to the Potteries and had planned to build a grandiose new church from well before the First World War. He actually accomplished his aim in the remarkable span of six years, 1925–30, but he was still fiddling with it when my father arrived on the scene and was promptly appointed Artistic Adviser, an exacting and thankless (and, needless to say, unpaid) task.

Father Ryan was thus in and out of our house constantly. I recognised him from the start as a great man, the first I had met, apart from my father. He was small, but stocky and muscular, fierce, beetle-browed, squinting, and he radiated authority, spiritual, temporal and, it seemed to me, supernatural. My father was a strong-minded man too, just as used to exercising authority, so they met as equals. He called my father 'Willie' but Daddy did not respond with 'Paddy' or even 'PJ' (the usual Irishism for men thus named). He was

always 'Father', or 'Your Reverence' if sarcasm was intended.
My father once summed up for me the genesis of our church:
'Little Paul, this is a case of enthusiasm compounded by
personal hubris. He wanted to outdo the Protestants of all
persuasions and build the biggest church in the district. So he
hired an architect called J. S. Brocklesby but had no intention
of following his designs. Old Brocklesby was a sensible fellow
who knew what was what, but His Reverence took him on a
tour of Europe – Italy, Germany and I don't know where – to
spot models to copy. And they got bigger and bigger.

'Brocklesby said, "Hold Hard, Father, it's not a cathedral,
you know." "Ah, sure," said he, "'twill be one day – and if it's
too big I shall fill it, the Potteries swarm with desperate souls
longing to be in Mother Church." "Well in that case,"
Brocklesby says, "you'll have to build a massive concrete
foundation for such a weight. That land is riddled with
mining passages only a few feet below the surface."'

It was true. The Potteries – the six towns of Tunstall,
Burslem, Hanley, Stoke, Fenton and Longton – stood in line
over one of the richest coalfields in England, the famous Black
Band. There were many seams, varying in thickness, but
reaching up to twenty-five feet. There was, they said, 'nothing
like it anywhere else'. It made the Potteries, enabling the
master potters to use up to twelve tons of coal for every ton
of fine ware, which required repeated firings. The coal was
cheap because it was right under their feet and the early
potters mined it themselves. These shallow workings, from
the sixteenth century onwards, posed terrible dangers to
anything built above them. So the towns were always
experiencing subsidence. Unlucky houses simply caved in and
were liable to vanish into a cavity. Rich people lived in houses
well away from the old seams.

'So listen to this, Little Paul,' said my father, 'it was decided, or His Reverence decided, to float the entire church on a raft of concrete. They poured in thousands of tons of the stuff, and when it hardened and settled they began to build. The locals said the raft would drag their houses out of alignment and perhaps it has. I don't know. Father Ryan laughed and said, "That's the *attraction* of the Church." He said, "Let's leave it all to Almighty God."

'Thus', said my father, 'they built. Father Ryan found a quarry in Derbyshire where they provided him with superb granite at a bargain price. He has a golden tongue, you know. But he couldn't decide whether he wanted a Gothic church or a baroque one. The truth is he wanted both. *And he had both!* He built a Gothic tower and he added a baptistry tower with a conical hat on it. Then he put up three domes in a row for the nave. Imagine the audacity of it! Brocklesby said, "Where do I put the high altar?" And His Reverence said, "Oh, I forgot the high altar. Build another dome." At that point old Brocklesby threw up his commission and stumped off in a huff. So Father Ryan built the half-dome himself. There you have it, Little Paul, a Gothic tower with three and a half domes. An architectural hybrid. An aesthetic mongrel. A piece of artistic nonsense. But, I'll grant you, a remarkable one.'

'I love it,' I said.

'That's a good boy,' said my father. 'Always love art which is honest in spirit and energetic in execution.'

'What kind of coat is a huff?'

'Eh?'

'What Mr Brocklesby stumped off in.'

My father laughed. 'All architects are in a huff, most of the time. Especially when dealing with clergymen.' So I was none the wiser.

I realised even at the time that Father Ryan had done something extraordinary. It is given to few men to build a

Father Ryan's great church

cathedral. All alone. Of course, he was not without help. Indeed, the help he secured was the most remarkable part of his achievement. It used to be believed that medieval cathedrals were the work of all the local population. Scrutiny of the records shows this was untrue: they were the work of expert master builders employing skilled workmen at going rates. But, in a few documented cases, locals helped. Father Ryan added to their number. He was not only his own architect but his own clerk of works. He sent out appeals to unemployed men to come and help him, 'at fair wages'. The response was enormous, and he could pick and choose.

He had a line-up, looked the likely candidates over, felt their muscles. 'You're a strong lad, what's your name? Stand over there. You with the red hair – are you from County Cork? Stand over there, Cork man. And you with the bold look, what's your name? Flannaghan? My mother's second cousin was a Flannaghan from Lismore. Stand over there.' He said, 'I'll have no hangdog shifty-looking men. Give me a straight look, and big hands and feet.' He would buy his labourers new boots if they lacked them; even a pair of corduroy trousers. He paid in cash, 'down to the last red penny', as he put it. The trade unions did not like it, but they would not risk a row with a popular cleric in those days, especially one providing work. The authorities turned a blind eye. That suited Father Ryan.

He had a blind eye himself – a glass one. How he lost an eye was never revealed: perhaps it was in 'the Troubles'. It was said that his glass eye was a cheap one, which fitted him ill and caused him pain; and that in the confessional he took it out, to ease himself. That, for me, added another terror to the confessional. I did not fancy, in the darkness, being alone with a man with an empty eye socket. But all he ever said to me, when I confessed, was 'Very good, child. Very good, child. Say three Hail Marys for the love of God. Now go, child, and let a Big Sinner in.'

He not only employed men without jobs. He also toured Europe to buy furnishings and decorations, or got local artists and craftsmen to make them. My father advised, found him suitable people, discussed their projects and helped to decide where the results were hung or placed. So Father Ryan was often at our house with some explosive scheme. My teatime was a convenient period for him and, while waiting for my father to arrive, he subjected me to intense scrutiny from his one blazing, brooding optic. 'Well, now, and what's that you're eating? Force is it called?' I preferred Force to Cornflakes. The packet had an athletic eighteenth-century squire leaping over a fence. He was called Sunny Jim. Father Ryan declared, 'To be sure, it looks forceful. Give thanks to Almighty God, Paul, for a full plate, there's many that lack it these terrible times. Depression they call it. There's no depression in heaven, for poverty often leads men to God.

And to hell, too, alas! What — are you going to eat a full round of toast after consuming that great dish of Force? Well, you'll be a giant in time. Now I'm a smallish man but I have the power in me. Fed on potatoes I was, on the farm in Galway. But there was no shortage of milk and butter, thanks be to God.'

He asked me to show him my hands, palms upwards. 'I'll not read your palm, that's sorcery and forbidden by the Holy Office. But I'll look at your fingers. Now, ye have pointed cushions in the top digits of your left hand. That shows ye'll be an artist, like your good father. Flat cushions signify a mere workman. Aye, ye'll do, young Paul. Eat up and grow strong, and serve God in art.'

Father Ryan's hubristic building plans, and his acquisitions of *objets d'art*, required money in perilous quantities. So there grew up a great subject referred to as 'The Debt'. It caused my father, who always paid bills by return of post, much concern. Father Ryan used to say, 'Ah, have done with your anxieties, Willie. I'll preach away The Debt.' At collection time, on Sundays, he was not above taking off his outer sacramental robes and presenting the box himself to each parishioner in turn, glaring at them with his one live eye. My father declared this to be 'unconscionable', but it worked. To be fair, Father Ryan never preached on this theme. In fact, he had only two sermons. If he was in a sunny mood he began, 'Consider the endless, ubiquitous, many-faceted, inexhaustible, unquantifiable goodness of Almighty God! How we feel it! How we enjoy it! How it envelops our lives! Let us give thanks!' This sermon was always short.

The other sermon began with the dread words 'Martin Luther!' and was a vituperative philippic against Protestantism in all its guises. This sermon was always long, for Father Ryan, having worked himself into a righteous rage, kept thinking of new iniquities to denounce and new arguments to drill into the bemused heads of parishioners. Sometimes he would start to get down from the pulpit but would be struck by a thought and climb up it again, for five minutes more of sectarian invective. Once or twice I even heard him carry on the sermon from the High Altar, before getting on with the mass.

The potters and colliers and their families took these things stoically. It was a place, a theatre indeed, where religious eccentricities were not only tolerated but admired and found an echo in simple hearts. It was from Tunstall, early in the nineteenth century, that William Clowes and Hugh Bourne, having quarrelled with the official Methodists of the town, struck out on to the nearby moors, inviting true Christians to follow, and held 'Camp Meetings' in the open. They called themselves Primitive Methodists and lived in tents or wood huts until accommodation was purchased in the town, usually in a private house turned into a chapel. This sect flourished throughout the Potteries and the desperate Thirties were a good time for them.

It was not uncommon to see groups of these men standing at street corners in Tunstall holding forth on Jesus, or singing one of Charles Wesley's hymns. My mother hurried me past. She disliked religious 'enthusiasm': it was 'presumptuous', a word which completely baffled me. In fact, she disliked hymns – I never heard her sing one. Her love of God was absolute and constant, right to the end of her long life; but she thought it wrong to demonstrate it in public. I was intrigued, however. Were they really 'primitive', something I associated with 'natives' in Africa, who wore paint, carried spears (like Anglo-Saxon warriors) and flourished delightful weapons called 'knobkerries'. And did they really live on Biddulph Moor? This was a sinister place I then knew only by repute.

It was said that the inhabitants were descended from 'Saracens', brought back as prisoners of war by the Crusaders. They spoke an impenetrable dialect and threw stones at strangers who invaded their fastnesses.

Other exotic forms of Protestantism raised their banners. There were eight forms of Methodism, each more 'pure' than the last. My father called them 'earthy'. Their boots, perhaps, were clogged with mud from the moors, I reasoned. There were the New Connection and the Old Wesleyans. The Kilhamites flourished. They awaited a Second Coming daily. The Bethel Evangelical Society operated from the ground floor of a Tunstall house, with a big poster in the window: 'Jesus is watching YOU!' I did not like that, oddly enough, although I prayed at night-time to Jesus to 'watch over me'. I dimly perceived there was an important distinction between 'is watching' and 'watch over'. There were many types of Baptists, said to be 'fierce'. The 'British Israelites' were few but came knocking at the door, like the Jehovah's Witnesses. My mother called them 'deluded' and 'moonstruck', making me think small portions of the moon had crumbled off and dealt them a powerful blow. The Catholic Apostles were not Catholic at all, I gathered, or Apostles either. The Christian Brethren were said to make their own clothes, for refined theological reasons. This did not impress. Was not my mother an expert knitter, turning out jumpers and whispering to herself 'knit one, purl two'? (In fact, she said, 'I am a poor knitter and do it as a penance.')

These sects waxed and waned in popularity. The Depression was a mixed blessing to them: it brought in the penitent but they came with empty hands. At the bottom of King William Street there was a grim reminder that times were hard. A Baptist faction, in 1929 as a stone plaque made clear, had started to build a grandiose chapel. One Alderman

Troughstone had laid the foundation stone. Its steel-and-concrete skeleton had been erected and a wodge of bricks put in place under its tower. Then funds had ceased and all work had been abandoned. The place had been derelict for several years when I discovered it. It was the haunt of a wild boy, a real Huckleberry Finn, called Lukey Lockgate, who sprang from nowhere whenever I visited the site. He had an iron on one leg and did not, I think, go to school. But he possessed a fund of information of the kind that did not come my way. 'Pa Snape was lude [drunk] last neet. Fell dun int' canal. Iz muz fished un ut.'

'Who's Pa Snape?'

'Dost thar not noow Snape? Is ed thrower at Barrington's.' (A thrower was a specialist potter.). Or again: 'Ma granfer's laid off at The Sytch bank. Er that's is muz sez it's curtains.' Men were, indeed, being laid off all the time. I had heard my father and His Reverence discuss it and shake weary heads. But what had that to do with curtains? Lukey could not enlighten me. Instead, as a mark of friendship, he offered me a partially sucked bull's-eye.

It was a sign of Father Ryan's militancy that he frequently organised processions from his church, midway through the principal mass on Sundays, banners displayed, the Blessed Sacrament carried aloft and all the congregation trudging behind, singing 'Faith of our Fathers'. This was a recusant anthem celebrating the steadfastness of papists during the penal times. It is forbidden now, in the interests of ecumenicalism, but then we sang it at the tops of our lungs, to annoy the Protestants. Father Ryan usually took the procession down King William Street, because of its name, infamous in Catholic annals, for William III was the victor of the Boyne, which killed the papists' cause in Ireland. (The fact that the street was named after William IV, the harmless 'Sailor King'

Sunday in the Potteries

who did nothing except sire innumerable bastards, was ignored by His Reverence.) A further reason was that the procession passed the site of the abandoned chapel before returning to Father Ryan's enormous church, which was finished and gloriously embellished, 'going great guns', as our curate put it – a splendid figure of speech which had me imagining Nelsonian cannons being dragged up the tower and bombarding the sullen Protestant mobs.

The curate, Father Corcoran, had a good deal to put up with, serving such an autocratic and ambitious master. But he took it all lightly. He was the most freckly man I have ever seen, 'a masterpiece of brown pigmentation', as my father put it. Even his hair was freckly. Gerard Manley Hopkins could have written a poem to him. Unlike Father Ryan, a country-man born on a farm with deep roots in the sad hills of

Galway, Father Corcoran was a Dubliner, a town lad, a sort of cockney with a brogue, what we would now call streetwise. He wisecracked, used slang, had a certain devil-may-care dash about him. What fascinated me about him was his war on cats.

'Do you and your family have trouble with the neighbouring toms?' he asked. 'Sure, they're a powerful tribe. And such a screeching and a yowling they put up at night has me destroyed. I get no sleep, I tell ye. The presbytery roof is their meeting place, the villains.'

'Why do they make a noise at night?' I asked.

'There's the why,' answered Father Corcoran, mysteriously. 'Sure, I don't let them get away with it. Last night I opened the window and pelted one with me shoes.'

'Your shoes?' I asked in alarm. 'What happened?'

'Ah, I missed once or twice, then I got the blagyard full pelt and shut him up for a spell. Sure, but I ran out of shoes. Not one left in the closet. I had the devil of a time, I can tell ye, Paul, gathering them up this morning.'

'My mother wouldn't let me throw my shoes at cats.'

'No more she would, bless her heart. But what I do with my own shoes is my own business and I will not tolerate the atrocious tyranny of those heathen cats. Sure Father Ryan sleeps through them all, he's a grand snorer.'

When I related this conversation to my mother, omitting the word 'devil', she said, 'He needs a good wife to look after him, the poor young man. Now, what am I saying? Sacerdotal celibacy is the bedrock of the Church.' She often said in self-rebuke, 'Never criticise the clergy.' But her robust common sense made this a hard rule to keep, though her disapproval took more the form of facial expressions, shrugs, impatient gestures of her graceful hands, than actual words.

When, many years later, in her nineties, she lay dying and I held her in my arms, I said. 'You'll go straight to heaven, Mother, you have never done wrong.'

She replied, 'I've often criticised the clergy.' They were, I think, her last words.

My mother criticised Father Ryan for imposing additional burdens on my father's bowed shoulders. She worried about him. On the day war was declared in August 1914, my father and his two brothers, Tom and Joe, and her three brothers, Joe, Jimmy and Wilf, had all volunteered, joining the same regiment, the Manchester battalion of the Artists' Rifles. My father had his Master's Certificate and could have got an immediate commission in the navy, who were desperately short of trained officers. But he chose to enlist with his friends and fight together as happy warriors in what all believed would be a short war. They were, of course, soon scattered, as the army machine ground them down and made a mockery of their patriotism. Tom was killed on the first day of the Battle of the Somme.

My father went through the whole tragic story of the Western Front, being wounded three times and gassed twice, once with the dreaded chlorine gas, which hurt his lungs badly. 'Your father has never been the same again,' said my mother. 'It will kill him, mark my words' – as indeed it did. Being nervous, impatient and a worrier, he smoked, as most men did then. He not only inhaled, he kept the cigarette in his mouth, while drawing, etching or lithographing – only in his Art Room, of course; he never smoked at school. It was a fearful habit, again shared by many men. He smoked Woodbines, too, to save money on a habit he deplored as self-indulgent and wasteful; his only sin, for he rarely drank, just on great feast days and then only a single glass of liqueur made by monks – Benedictine or Chartreuse. Occasionally, being bronchial and warned by Dr Halpin, he switched to 'medicinal cigarettes', which Clare called bonfires because that's what they smelt like, but then it was back to 'the gaspers'. His cough became habitual and harrowing, and frightened me. My mother said it was 'a graveyard cough'.

So she wanted him to rest when he came home from his exacting duties at his Art School. But Father Ryan was always at him: to come and approve a new crucifix, carved in Bavaria, 'a piece of workmanship to charm the angels, Willie, real nails and blood coming out of the wounds in cataracts'. Or to touch up a new statue of St Theresa, 'just a dot or two of gold paint is what's needed'. Or to look at a catalogue of reliquaries, just arrived from Madrid. My father designed side altars and railings, he painted a backdrop to a pietá, a loathsome task for him, as he disliked fresco. He disliked working in oils, too — he was essentially a graphite-and-wash artist — but this was often required to improve a holy image His Reverence had bought ridiculously cheaply in a Bruges or Ghent junk shop. In a way my father enjoyed these tests of his craftsmanship, for he was an improviser of genius and loved a challenge to his ingenuity. Sometimes he summoned a talented lad or girl from his school to help. He had an atelier in the church crypt, which he took me to, which was more like a Renaissance studio than his own tidy Art Room at home.

One way or another, I was never absent from the great church for long. I loved the enormous domes, gazing up at their pale heavenly blue. The angels, with golden sandals, popped up everywhere, fluttering about the nave like birds. Some of the benches were carved with scenes of nature — otters, foxes and badgers at play — and men making pots. They were the work of a gifted local craftsman-artist called 'Chisel' O'Keefe. My father took me to see him chipping away. He was an old man with a green eye-shade. All I remember is his saying to me,

'Keep your tools Sheffield-sharp.' The bells were cast under Father Ryan's personal supervision, at Shelton foundry, an enviable occasion considered too dangerous for me to witness. One, a high treble, was called Paul: my father joked it was after me, not the Saint. On Sundays I tried to distinguish his shrill note amid the brazen cacophony. Father Ryan also persuaded the great Spode works to make him ritual pottery vessels of alarming size, which were placed on the High Altar until the bishop, a nervous fellow who usually gave our pastor a wide berth, had his secretary protest that they were 'irregular'. Father Ryan threatened 'to write to the Pope', a frequent menace of his, but the big dishes went into the presbytery, to the consternation of Mrs Brownsword, the housekeeper.

So Father Ryan carried on decorating and improving his cathedral. My mother often had him to a meal, and Father Corcoran too, not trusting Mrs Brownsword to feed them properly. My mother had a saying: 'Never let a week go by without giving a priest a good dinner.'

'What about nuns?' I asked.

'Oh, nuns can look after themselves. They're always in and out of the convent kitchen, nibbling. Besides, nuns are faddy these days.' Her authority for these disparaging remarks was her aunt, or perhaps great-aunt, Reverend Mother Mary Winifred Boulton, a tall, thin lady, rattling with rosary beads and scapular, who ran 'a house of nuns with an iron rod'. On her rare visits I looked for this iron rod but it was not there: instead, an umbrella which would not have shamed Mrs Gamp.

So Father Ryan was often sat at the table and his *obiter dicta* resonate in my memory. 'If you see a boy running, whip him. For if he's not running away from trouble, he's running into it.' 'Mr Baldwin, I'll allow, has horse sense.'

'What's horse sense, Father?'

'It's the sense that makes them never bet on a horse.' He had been in New York. 'Now, that's a terrible place. I'd not been there five minutes when I saw a priest strolling down Fifth Avenue, bold as brass, smoking a cigar. A *cigar*, I tell you, in the *streets*. Oh, that was a frightful thing to see. If a priest smokes a cigar at one end, he'll find the devil smoking it at the other.'

My mother, seeing my alarm, added hastily, 'Father doesn't mean it literally, Paul, but metaphorically.' That did not satisfy, but silenced, me. I was beginning to know a bit about metaphors – they were lies grown-ups were allowed to tell.

Father Ryan, though much older, outlived my father. He died in 1951 and it was said his funeral procession was five miles long. In those days, funerals were public events and scrutinised carefully. Men stood in the streets and took off their hats until the hearse passed. The mourners, men anyway, walked to the cemetery 'as a sign of respect'. Six bishops were present on this occasion, or so it was reported to my mother, who had long and thankfully left the district. Edifying as such a turnout was, there was some scandalised whispering when Father Ryan's Will became public. He left, it seemed, £50,000, an enormous sum then, and all to his family in Ireland. My mother, paradoxically, was gratified by this news. It confirmed her low views of Irish clergy. Still, he had also left a remarkable church.

My father drew it often, with its high towers and three and a half domes. He had an engaging habit of making rapid but often beautifully detailed sketches of buildings and skylines in the margins of any book he happened to be reading. He thus adorned many volumes of Thomas Hardy, his favourite novelist. I recently came across a copy of Richard Jefferies's *Wild Life in a Southern County*, similarly annotated with sketches of Tunstall in great profusion. He also drew the church on large sheets of fine cartridge paper: but all these were sold at the time, as indeed were nearly all of his finished topographical works, so that I possess only a few. He loved drawing churches, and did them with great care and accuracy. For a time he had a regular contract with a Catholic weekly newspaper to draw all the suitable churches of the Midlands, each of which was reproduced in line over half a page. This was arduous and exacting work, and after he had done about a hundred he had to give it up.

When I was five or six, he took me occasionally with him on expeditions to draw a building not too far away. These were, to me, gratifying occasions, for he encouraged me to draw the same subject and commended – and helped – my efforts. I always kept close in my heart on these trips whatever he said to me. One thing in particular I remember: 'You have a certain talent, Little Paul, I am bound to admit. But don't become an artist. Bad times are coming for our profession. I foresee that frauds like Picasso will rule the roost for the next fifty years. So do something else.' Well, he was right, wasn't he? Most of his remarks, however, were addressed to himself, *sotto voce*, as he drew and scrutinised, rubbed out or sharpened his pencils.

Many were technical. 'An 8H [pencil] is a true graphite, straight from Borrowdale.' 'Turner said, always respect your paper. Now what exactly did he mean by that?' Later: 'He meant don't always be rubbing out. Think hard before you make a stroke.' Then: 'Turner also said don't put important things in the corners.' He often criticised the building. 'That pinnacle must have been carved by a lunatic. Impossible to draw.' Or: 'The whole of the chancel is slightly out of alignment. The master builder was drunk.' Or: 'The church looks like a Methodist chapel.'

But some of his mutterings had nothing to do with art. 'Marvell is a finer poet than Dryden.' 'Never miss a legitimate opportunity to kiss a pretty woman.' 'Czechs make the best dentists.' 'The Horn is overrated for bad weather, especially if you take the southern route.' '*The Woodlanders* is Hardy's best book, for landscape anyway.' He turned to me: 'By the time you're grown up, Little Paul, everyone will be driving in motor cars and life will not be worth living.' A favourite topic was cities: he had seen them all and drawn many. 'Valparaiso is a true Victorian city. But then so is Melbourne.' Later: 'And San Francisco, of course. Sorry I missed that grand earthquake.' 'Dublin is a dirty city. The Liffey is the colour of dark chocolate.' 'Nancy is the most beautiful city in France. Pure rococo.' 'Now Cracow is a fine place. Polish girls make bad wives but good mistresses.' 'No one wants to go to Rangoon twice.' 'I've never known a Finn tell a lie.' 'A Dutch woman will always cook you a good meal. But their breath smells.' 'Churchill was a fool to quarrel with Baldwin.' And so on, for his concentration on his drawing was prodigious – visible in the intensity of his features, and his eyes flickering from building to drawing board and back again almost every second. Often he did not remember what he had muttered.

I was interested in his remark about Polish ladies making good mistresses, which to me meant schoolteachers. I asked, 'Do they use the blackboard a lot?'

'Eh?'

'The Polish mistresses. You said they were good.'

'Did I? Ha, ha, ha. What did you think I meant, Little Paul?'

'I wondered if they had a red jewel eye in the back of their head, like Miss Travis.'

'Alethia Travis as a mistress, I like that,' said my father. 'I must tell your mother that.' Then, 'On reflection, better not.'

We failed to get to the bottom of this problem. But, as a child, I was happy to live with mysteries and conundrums, which seemed to me a natural part of things. In church we were always being told of mysteries which could not, need not and ought not to be explained. To be baffled occasionally was to me a small price to pay for the privilege of having either of my parents talk to me with the freedom they did. I took it for granted but, at the same time, I knew I was lucky.

My father's company was not at all like my mother's. I loved them both, but he inspired awe. I could detect my mother's emotions and forward thoughts (and *arrière-pensées*) with perfect accuracy by minute observation of her face and hands, her whole body. I have never met anyone to whom the term 'body language' applied so perfectly. She often spoke with her body just before she spoke with her tongue; or, indeed, when she was designedly mute. My father was less penetrable and, I think, less consistent. With my mother I spoke, if I could find the words, with total lack of restraint. With my father I felt I had to be a little circumspect. He had the reputation, in his school, of being a disciplinarian. Even in the family he was thought to be strict. My elder siblings told me so. They spoke darkly of being threatened with, or even actually receiving, 'a good thrashing'.

Here was another puzzle. A thrashing was presumably painful. How then could it be good? Perhaps the phrase was just a deterrent. Clare and Elfride often said that I was in danger of being 'marred' (a lovely term of my mother's) because the household rules had been made so much easier since their day and any punishment less strict. But I do not believe that either of them – or Tom, for that matter – was ever beaten or even slapped. We were a family in which such physical acts would have seemed quite out of place. Words were our system of government, of rewards and penalties. But my parents used them with great justice and effect. All the same, I was in awe of my father. His approval was the highest accolade. His disappointment — he used the words 'You have disappointed me, Little Paul', with dread and sadness — were punishment indeed. Pleasing him became the central object of my life.

CHAPTER FOUR

Picture Palace and The Sytch

MY LIFE WAS not confined to the park and the church. Far from it. First there was Arthur Machin. Arthur was our milkman. He was tall, burly, in his twenties, with the reddish-brown complexion that proclaims farming stock. God had graced him with a sunny disposition. Indeed, I don't think I have ever known anyone who so consistently, wholly and engagingly kept up his spirits – and mine too.

He appeared promptly at eight o'clock every morning with his pony and trap. My mother and I would hear his cheerful 'Milk-Oh!' and go out with the jug. He would take off the lid of his big silver-coloured churn in the back of the trap, plunge his ladle deep in the fresh, creamy milk and bring it up foaming. My mother approved of Arthur. 'He is everything a farmer's boy ought to be,' she said and would then sing softly, 'I am a farmer's boy-ho-hoy, I *am* a farmer's boy.'

Arthur liked me, too, and I liked him. 'Hop up, Paul Bede,' he would say, using my second name, which pleased me. 'I'll take thee round the 'ouses.' His pony, Arabella, whom he loved passionately, was what he called 'a high stepper'. 'She belonged t'family of the Duke at Trentham,' he said to me. 'But she used t'bolt, don't noa why. So me dad gorrer chip [cheap].' Arabella knew exactly when to start and stop, and needed no driving at all. ' 'Er'll never bolt now,' said Arthur. 'She's nervous-like and needs a firm master but' – he pronounced it 'buoout' – 'she likes me, 'er does.' And why not? Everyone liked Arthur.

'Buoout', he said, 'it makes no sense 'aving pony-'n'-trap nar [now]. I tell thee, Paul Bede, this is t'age of motor. Ah say t'Dad, gi' me a van and ah can dubble the round. Why throw good milk awa when thee can sell ut? Ah could go reet rand Chell'um all in same tum [time].'

'But I love Arabella,' I said, 'going on your round here with her and she loves it too.'

'I dessay, Paul Bede, buoout, life's not all love and kisses, tha knowst, it's wurk and profit and lukin aheed. Ma dad's wuss than thee, 'e's a *reactionary*' (a word just coming into popular use as the Thirties, 'that low, dishonest decade', got into its ideological stride).

The Machins' farm, Moor Edge, a mile away, had been in the family for generations. Arthur would take me there occasionally, when he dumped his empty milk churns and picked up new ones. There was a chorus of howls and yelps as the dogs rushed out – Sarah, the sheepdog, a collie, Laskar, the brown terrier, and Golden Girl, the beautiful Labrador who guarded the farmyard. Arthur promised to take me ratting one day, in the barns, where Laskar was in charge of operations. But my mother forbade it. She was squeamish about killing things, even rats, though she could never bring herself to pronounce the name. She would not willingly kill a fly, a distaste I have inherited. Arthur was philosophical: 'Ladies is delicate-like.' His father was like Arthur: jovial. But he had 'bin in t'trenches', like my father, and had seen modern horrors. His affections were back in the nineteenth century when 't'old wooman were on t'trone and Lud Sosby [Lord Salisbury] were in control. We 'ad our playses, then, us an' all, and were gratified. Now it's all picture palaces, eh, Arthur?'

'Vans, Dad, when um us going to get t'van, eh?'

'That'll be day,' his father answered. 'Dost want to bankrupt un, eh? I'll van thee.'

Mrs Machin presided over a vast old-fashioned kitchen where the farmhands got their dinner at noon. It was full of good smells and hung with hams and cheeses, and festooned with ancient cooking implements, a musket and hunting horns. Her daughter Dora and the milkmaid Pattie helped her. There was always a titbit for me: a currant bun with whipped cream in it or a piece of arny-cake, a heavy sweet-meat of treacle and honey. Mrs Machin would say, 'Thy curls, Paul Bede, are the light of my life, thou cherib.' And Dora and Pattie always gave me a kiss each. I was to find, later in life, and especially at boarding school, that having curly bright-red hair was a handicap, a source of prejudice and a stigma. But in my infancy it was a bright arrow to hearts, especially female ones, and a signal to be pressed against buxom bosoms.

Arthur would take me up Queen's Avenue, past the church and round it, and then down the alleyway at its back, calling at garden doors all the way. With my sisters, however, I would go further up into Tunstall, past the crossroads. There, King William Street, where the poor lived, opened upon the left and Victoria Road, down which the villas of the well-to-do reposed in ample gardens, stretched on the right, along the south side of the park. At this point Queen's Avenue ended, the road crossed the railway line (with Tunstall Station on the left), then became The Boulevard. Who thought of giving this grandiose name to a nondescript stretch of road leading into Tunstall proper I do not know. Pronouncing it was quite beyond the locals. They called it Bolvey Yard, which puzzled strangers.

First point of call, on the left just where the path down to the black hole of Tunstall Station began, was Shrigley's, a 'superior' sweetshop, which sold boxes of chocolates from Terry's and Rowntree's, Quality Street Assortment and sweets from exotic places like Perugia and Brussels. A refined lady was in charge, who did not welcome children unless they were 'well-spoken'. We qualified but boys with smutty faces and girls with running noses – a universal test of poverty, then, for such children never had hankies – were chased away: 'Off my premises, you impudent creatures!' We never bought there, unless a windfall had come our way; but we could look.

Across the road was Mr Greasley's, the barber's shop. He did men on weekdays, boys on Saturdays; girls never. I did not like him. I suppose he was exasperated by having to cut the hair of other dirty boys for a mere tuppence. He certainly behaved as if he regarded us as one remove worse than dogs. Indeed, nowadays he would have run a dog parlour. You had to wait in a smelly, shuffling line on hard benches with nothing to look at, for comics were forbidden and talking above whispers suppressed with ferocity. When your turn came Mr Greasley would say 'Next! Sharply, there!' and slam a board across the arms of his barber's chair, so that you sat high up and exposed. 'Now, then,' he said, 'keep as still there as an Eastern idol!' Then he would whizz round with his patent clippers, giving you a short-back-and-sides, army fashion (he had learned his trade in the North Staffs Fusiliers). There came a time – I remember it – when technology caught up and Mr Greasley's clippers were replaced by an electrical machine. He did not at first master this contraption and dealt one painful nicks, even drawing blood on one occasion, then dabbing the wound with an agonising swab of iodine, the universal medicament and antiseptic.

My mother dreaded these periodic visits to Greasley's almost as much as I did. Her fears were twofold. First, that he would smear my hair with a hefty blob of brilliantine or similar 'cream', then almost universally employed by males to make their hair slick and smart. She regarded 'hair oil', as she called it, as the depths of vulgarity and degradation. Second, she was even more terrified that I would acquire, not from Greasley's implements but from 'rough boys' sitting on the bench, waiting, what Arthur Machin referred to jokingly as 'town livestock'. These came in two varieties: 'nits', verminous eggs, which stuck to your hair and, far worse, 'wogs', live headlice which ranged freely, made you itch and bred nits with speed and in enormous quantities. When I came back from Greasley's my mother would anxiously search my head for signs of an invasion, fortunately without ever finding any. There was a special fine-toothed comb for this purpose. Periodic, still more habitual, possession of town livestock was the hallmark of working-class status and/or poverty. Middle-class mothers were particularly anxious to maintain their class status in this respect. My hair was constantly washed as a precaution, even though my mother whispered darkly, 'The creatures' (she could not bring herself to use the word 'wogs', though 'nits' was just permissible) 'love clean hair.'

When I was young, my red-gold curls attracted attention. People would stop in the streets and congratulate whoever was with me – mother or sisters – on 'such a fine cherub like' and run their often far from clean hands through my hair. My mother hated this. I was sometimes presented with a penny, even with a sixpence. But this was always refused on my behalf (to my concealed annoyance) or if it was pressed into my eager palm, I was made to return it. My mother said firmly, 'They can't really afford it and you don't need it.' But Potteries people were generous, especially when in liquor. A drunken man once gave me a sixpence 'for being an angel' and no one noticed. So I kept it in my trouser pocket, where it was discovered. Asked to explain, I said I had found it: my first conscious lie. Even so, it was impounded and put in a tin post-office box placed out of reach on the kitchen mantelpiece.

Nits are still with us, I believe, and outbreaks are indignantly recorded even in upper-middle-class circles. So in that respect things have not radically changed. But in those days the working class smelt. In the Potteries I doubt if one in ten working-class families had a bathroom, though the authorities were doing everything in their power to build new housing estates with three bedrooms in each home, a bathroom, proper kitchen and downstairs indoor lavatory. Those without bathrooms had no running hot water either: it had to be boiled in a pot or kettle on the kitchen fire. They could not afford dry cleaning. A shirt had to last a week, a vest (all wore them) a fortnight or a month. One reason I preferred girls to boys was that girls did not, as a rule, smell. Boys did, of a mixture of sweat, urine and indeterminate grime.

My mother said that Miss Travis regularly had cleanliness inspections of the boys' class and paid particular attention to the backs of their necks. 'Grey with dirt' was a favourite expression of hers; or 'black with ingrained dirt'. Sometimes she would address the class: 'Do you know what I call you? The Great Unwashed.' Miss Travis was not above dragging a particularly grimy boy by his hair into the school kitchen and scrubbing him in the sink, something which would now earn her instant dismissal and a prison term. I discovered early that most filthy boys were ashamed of their dirt – poor Lukey in particular – but did not know what to do about it. Poverty was then shameful and dirt was its commonest external sign. Boys hated wearing old, dirty clothes, handed down, darned and patched, rarely cleaned in any way.

One place, a little further up the Bolvey Yard from Mr Greasley's shop, where dirt was palpable, was the library,

where I made myself at home at the earliest possible opportunity, even before I could read; an easy thing to do, as my
sisters used it constantly. Miss Cartlich, in charge of the desk,
was another authoritarian – life was full of tyrants in those
days – who regarded boys with particular suspicion. She
disliked old men too. They came into the library to get out of
the cold and to rest their weary legs, for their daughters-in-
law would not tolerate them at home during the day, 'getting
under my feet'. They had no money – literally, not a penny –
for any form of entertainment and therefore could only walk
the streets aimlessly. The reading room of the public lending
library was thus a winter garden of rest for them. But of
course they fell asleep and Miss Cartlich, who regularly visited
it to detect sleepers, would then wake them up and escort
them off the premises, if necessary taking a hand to their
collar. 'Out, out, out!' she would say, 'I'll have no men here
snoring in my reading room.' If they could stay awake,
however, and pretend to be reading, the old men were safe.

They smelt powerfully, not a little-boy smell but a sickly-
sweet geriatric pong, composed of tobacco, beer stains,
chronic bodily complaints and sheer weariness. Their feet, in
particular, stank of unwashed socks and ancient shoes barely
holding together. Women never sat in the reading room. Old
women were kept at home, doing menial tasks, scrubbing,
polishing, whitening the front doorstep, washing in tubs,
ironing with heavy pieces of cast iron heated almost red-hot
at the open fire. But old men, past earning and good for
nothing, were expected to stay out in daylight hours.

The library thus sounds a dreary place, but to me it was full
of excitement. There was an enormous coloured print of the
Duke of Wellington shaking hands with Marshal Blücher
after the Battle of Waterloo, dead, wounded and the debris of
battle all around. And another, by Copley, of Nelson dying at

Trafalgar in the cockpit of HMS *Victory*. Both these wonderful pictures had the fascinating detail boys love. There was another of Queen Elizabeth knighting Sir Francis Drake, and the mortally wounded Wolfe lying, victorious, on the Heights of Abraham above Quebec. I liked also Chatham (I knew that was another name for Pitt the Elder) dying in the House of Lords and the Mayor of London Killing Wat Tyler with the Boy King Richard II looking on. All these scenes are engraved on my memory until this day and will fade only when my eyes shut for ever.

Before I read, or read fervently, I would search the books on the shelves for pictures, of pirates, 'natives', Chinamen, Eskimos, tattooed heads from New Zealand, the heroes of Ossian, the *Nibelungenlied*, Arthurian Knights, Norse sagas and other grand tales. If I had paper I would copy them. Usually I committed them to memory: a growing cast of fantastically dressed and hirsute figures to put into my sketching repertory. So I loved the library and left reluctantly when my sisters had chosen their books.

Even more exciting and further down the Bolvey Yard, on the opposite side, was Tunstall's first, and for long its only, cinema. This was called Barber's Picture Palace and was the personal property of Tunstall's most eminent citizen, Alderman George Barber. Mr Barber was a character, a card, on a scale to make Arnold Bennett's Potteries heroes seem feeble creatures. He had been born in a workhouse, dreadful places in his day, where children born there were deposited in orphanages and frequently died in infancy. He was a fighter. A chancer. An entrepreneur. Indeed, he was a genuine hero, on a smaller scale but of the same type as his older contemporary, Andrew Carnegie. Like Carnegie, he wrote his autobiography, *From Workhouse to Lord Mayor*, in which those who are interested in rags-to-riches can find a classic Dick

Whittington story and much curious period detail. Mr Barber was universally admired; not envied – the Potteries were never envious – but looked up to as a living, working model of what grit and energy could achieve, starting from nothing. 'That man is a wonder,' they would say. ''E started with nowt and new [now] 'e's worth millions. Can'st imagine?' ''E could eat 'is dinner off gold playt if 'e wushed.' Or: 'See that reet 'and of 'is? That 'and as shaken ter 'and of Prince of Wales.' He was said to be 'personally known and recognised by the King'. He had travelled. 'Knowst thou that dictator-chap in Germany? Aye, 'Itler. The Alderman knows 'im. I'm telling thee, that man's a wonder. 'E's met Stalin, the Bolshevik king. 'E met the Yank, wotsit, Ruoooosevelt – aye!'

One story about Mr Barber struck me forcibly. If there was one thing the potters loved, it was boiled ham. They ate it in great quantities when they could afford it. They ate the fat too. That disgusted me. The large slabs of cold fat that invariably accompanied a tasty slice of ham was an abomination to me and my mother, bless her good heart and sense, never forced me to eat it. Now Mr Barber, as a leading personality of the Potteries, played a notable role when they celebrated the fifteen-year anniversary of the amalgamation of the six towns into one county borough, which had occurred in 1910. This event, which also marked the emergence of Stoke-on-Trent as a city, took place in 1925 and on the culminating day the King and Queen attended a sumptuous luncheon, or dinner as it was called by everyone. Mr Barber, as he deserved, was put next to Queen Mary, our poker-stiff model of decorum. She shared my distaste for cold ham fat and carefully pushed hers to one side of her plate, concealing it under a neat pile of less important detritus. But the eagle eye of the Alderman was on to her and it. ''Ere, Your Majesty, if thee dustna want that luvly fat, *I'll* eat it!' And he stretched out a long fork, pronged it, brought it back to his plate and ate it in triumph. Queen Mary, after an instantly raised eyebrow and rattle of her six-strand pearl neck collar, smiled and subsequently pronounced the Alderman 'a hero'. I endorsed this accolade: anyone who not only ate his own ham fat but positively volunteered to eat somebody else's, too, was certainly a paladin in my eyes. I admired the Queen, too, for her taste.

Mr Barber was involved in many activities. But the cinema came closest to his heart and he saw himself as a pioneer in what, by the mid-1930s, was undoubtedly the most powerful cultural force in the world. At the end of the war, when purpose-built cinemas were rare, he had bought an old army lorry, converted it into a mobile film van and toured round the Potteries. This proved highly successful. With the proceeds he built Barber's Picture Palace. I say 'built', but he probably adapted it from an old music hall or theatre. It had a lot of red plush and brass bars separating the different sections. The entrance hall had a flourish of curved staircase leading up to the posher seats on the first floor. It looked as if it was designed to present Mae West slinking down it in a long corset dress with a feather boa. Potted palms were set about in brass tubs, themselves encased in Spode ware. In fitting out and embellishing his palace Mr Barber had drawn heavily on the products of the Potteries. For the pot-banks produced not only tableware but tiles of every description. Mr Barber was particularly proud of his Ladies and Gents lavatories, 'sumptuously tiled from head to foot', as he put it.

Mr Barber, as I remember him, was short and stocky, a bantam cock, with grizzly hair, pink face and bushy moustache. He looked a bit like Lloyd George. His eyes twinkled, he had a merry step and he often wore bow ties with his bowler. He liked to be in charge. Indeed, he was another of those authority figures who peopled my childhood. All owners of places of public entertainment in those days, from pubs to football grounds, decided who would be let in and who not. On weekdays the chief cashier, Miss Clayworthy, exercised this function at the palace.

But on Saturday afternoon Mr Barber took charge himself, for at the Saturday afternoon showing there was a special children's programme and he personally supervised the tightening of discipline this required. 'Boys,' he thundered, standing plumb middle of the entrance. 'Boys! I'll have no fighting or scuffling or horseplay. I'll refine you! I'll ketch and put you in line! Form a neat queue to the office, with your pennies ready. That's reet. No spitting! Who's the low boy that spit? Reet – no room for thee, thou rascal! Turn him away, turn him away! And look 'ere – who said *thee* could cum in? Go back wum [home] and wash thy dirty face! I'll admit no unwashed boys in my palace, that's flat! Dust 'ear?'

Boys were hauled out of the queue and ejected for various reasons, not only dirt. 'Ah've seen thee before, thou chimpanzee, and ah doan't like thy tricks – turn him away, dost 'ear, Miss Clayworthy? Aye, and thou wilt not enter neither, young shiftless. Gerroutofit!' He thus stood there, like St Peter, custodian of the pearly gates, dividing sheep from goats. If he saw a well-dressed little girl, he would direct her to be shown upstairs, to the tuppence-halfpenny seats, though she had only a penny. This favouritism benefited me on more than one occasion. 'There's a nice, clean, tidy boy! Good afternoon, Sir, it's a pleasure to entertain you. Miss Clayworthy, take this young gent's penny and send 'im up to the two-and-a-halves – dost 'ear?' So up I went, and sat with a less unsavoury collection of children, in one of the wings on either side by the real posh seats, in the mid-balcony, which cost sixpence.

We got good value for our money, even without this arbitrary upgrading: a big picture, a B-feature, the Movietone or Pathé-Gaumont News, sometimes both, a short funny – Laurel and Hardy, Harold Lloyd, Old Mother Riley or the Three Stooges, and a Mickey Mouse too. No advertising, unless Mr Barber was anxious to promote some local cause, activity or person on whom his gracious eye of favour currently dwelt. He sometimes wrote out the scores of local football teams and showed them on the screen as the afternoon drew to a close. In a good mood, he would take the tray from the ice-cream girl and distribute its contents free, but again on an arbitrary basis. In a bad mood he would address the audience. 'Now look 'ere. Ah've 'urd say that they call this palace the Flea Pit! Not in my 'earing they dusn't. This is not a flea pit! This glorious palace is scrubbed out and 'oovered and dusted, and fumigated every week. Ask Mrs Snape and 'er team of cleaning ladies! If there ever are fleas in this place, 'oo brought them? You did! They doan't grow 'ere, tha knowst! Fleas! I'll flea you!'

Alderman Barber is long gone and almost forgotten, I suppose, for local heroes like he was do not figure in the *Dictionary of National Biography.* His palace is a bingo hall or was when last heard of. Even in his own day – I remember it well – a new cinema was opened in Tunstall, the Ritz, with a proper sloping floor specially designed for cinema showing. My mother, who would never set foot in Barber's Palace – 'nothing but fleas and smoke there' – was willing to take me to the Ritz. But the Palace had more flavour. You never knew what would happen if Mr Barber was around. He completed the performance with an *impromptu*.

The rest of Tunstall was undistinguished, with one exception. The Boulevard led eventually into the town Square. There was a Town Hall on the bottom side of the Square, a daunting, echoing place inside, and the scene of a painful episode in my life as my time in the Potteries drew to a close — it will be described in its place. Behind this building, and in some way part of it, was the town Market Hall and that was of great interest to me. With or without my sisters I visited it every Saturday without fail. Pocket money was scarce. My pocket money was only threepence even when I was nine. It is true there were other sources of income: relatives, friends of my parents and visitors would occasionally dole out a sixpence or even a shilling. But, in general, every penny was carefully considered before spent. So I looked for the cheapest places and the market stalls supplied them. They had 'broken sweets'. They had second-hand toys. They had cheap stuff from Germany and Japan, which reputable toyshops would not condescend to sell.

Moreover, the market had atmosphere. Its light systems were mysterious and shifting. Its stallholders were rough, jovial men and women, who spoke the Potteries or Moorland dialects in their coarsest forms, joked and swore with tremendous abandon, and reeked of beer and spirits. They made fun of me because of my curly 'carrot top'. 'Canna warm me 'ands at thy 'ead?' they would joke. But they were generous and devil-may-care. They would always offer me sweets. They might knock a penny off the price of a toy or even look around for a damaged one and give it me free. They were said to get drunk every Saturday night after the market closed and never to go to church on Sunday. In fact, they were outside the social system of Tunstall, which was based very largely on church or chapel affiliation. They were outside and perhaps they saw in me another outsider, who lived in Tunstall but whose thoughts were elsewhere. Anyway, I liked these rough folks; loved them in some cases. Most of them seemed to be called Sneyd, a common name in Tunstall, for the Sneyds had once owned the whole district and built Keele Hall.

I liked Potteries names, which often had deep local resonances. Some came from towns, which had been villages until the late eighteenth century: Biddulphs, Hanleys, Burslems, even a Tunstall or two. Others came from rivers: Churnets and Manifolds, Doves, Sow and Hamps. There was a family called Loggerhead and another Mucklestone — both villages not far away. Snape was another common name, Twomlow, Greatbatch, Shrigley, Oldfield, Greenhow, Snyde, Cowbridge and Brownfield.

The Town Hall was in the High Street, which opened on to a square, sloping upwards to the crest of the ridge, which ran right through the Potteries and was the source of its wealth, for it contained not only coal but china clay, ironstone and much else, all near the surface and easy to dig. The Square and its adjuncts were an amazing collection of incongruous buildings, including small houses, turned into shops, which had been part of the original village and had not long lost their thatched roofs and black-and-white sides of timber and clutch. Religion flourished to a degree inconceivable now. Just on the other side of the Square, below the summit of the ridge, were three Wesleyan chapels, all professing finely differentiated versions of the Methodist faith.

A house near the Square was the haunt of Sandemanians or Glasites. This weird sect had been started in the mid-eighteenth century by a Presbyterian Scotch elder, author of a famous tract called *Letters on Theron and Aspaslio* (1757). He married a buoyant lady called Catherine, daughter of John Glas, who founded a sect of his own. I know nothing of the theology of the Sandemanians, or the Glasites for that matter, or why they turned from the established churches. What interested me, at the time, was being told they held a

The Potteries: God and Mammon

ceremony every Sunday, attended by the entire congregation, and washed each other's feet. Feet tended to be smelly in the Potteries, as I have already hinted, and the source of endless coarse jokes. The Sandemanians, as I glimpsed them through the windows of their 'chapel', struck me as rather solemn, and the idea of these starched-collar gentlemen and heavily corseted ladies getting down to scrubbing each other's feet in pails of soapy water was intriguing. Alas, the weekly foot-washing ceremony took place when we were in our own church, so I never saw it, and rumour has it that the Sandemanian church is now 'extinct'.

Less funny to me, indeed, not funny at all – rather frightening, in fact – was a church or house in the High

Street, near the Square, which had just been opened. This was occupied by Spiritualists, who were going great guns, as Father Corcoran would say, in the 1930s. They already had one church in nearby Piccadilly Street, but the popularity of the cult – perhaps due to distraught parents and fiancées trying to get in touch with men killed in the Great War – made a second and grander establishment necessary. My sister Clare told me that Spiritualists 'conjured up the dead and spoke to them'. Elfride, more pious, said, 'It is forbidden to talk about them.' My mother laughed and said, 'Great-Aunt Aggie Lloyd became a Spiritualist before the war and a man called Mr Myerscough got all her money off her. Serve her right, she was always a flibbertigibbet, or so Aunt Seed said.' The windows of 41a High Street were closely curtained, even in the daytime, and I never saw anyone go in or out. I imagined dead people, dressed like mummies with ancient flapping bandages, wandering about inside. Possibly attended by flibbertigibbets who, Elfride said, were a kind of devil, 'not to be the subject of general conversation', a phrase that she had picked up, I suspect, from her religious teacher, Sister Mary Magdalen.

Devils were real to me. Father Ryan had said, from the pulpit and possibly with reference to Martin Luther's illicit wife whom he had described as 'an escaped nun', that vanity was a sure way to arouse the devil; and that 'any human creature who looks in a mirror for more than twenty-five seconds is liable to find the devil looking over her shoulder, grinning fiendishly at another captive soul'. I think it true to say that I have never looked in a mirror, by my own choice, for more than ten seconds, let alone twenty-five, so that is one moral lesson well learned.

The old Town Hall had been in the centre of the Square but had been knocked down, when the new and more spacious Town Hall was built, and replaced by a clock tower. My father said this clock was 'an inferior job' to the one in the park. Not only did it lack 'nobility', his favourite turn of phrase, as it was Sir Edward Elgar's, but it had a 'nonsensical abutment'. He also criticised the new Town Hall, as 'an abdication of architectural principle and not worth drawing'. But he liked the Jubilee Buildings, put up in 1889 to mark Queen Victoria's Golden Jubilee and now containing the public baths, scene of Polly's transvesticism. He said they were 'a good effort' with 'uncommon ideas'. Around and on all sides of the big municipal building were funny little streets of what my father called 'cottages'. These were put up in the 1820s, he said, as 'superior housing for the industrious poor', chiefly potters, by the Tunstall Building Society. Each two-storey house had front and back rooms on both storeys, with a privy and ashpit in the walled yard at the back. They were for immigrants from the surrounding moors, lured by high wages in the proliferating pot-banks, and seemed luxurious at the time: these rows of terraces formed what was optimistically called Paradise Street. My father said, 'They are pretty and neighbourly. They are sure to be pulled down soon.' They were.

My father also said, 'Now, Little Paul, I am going to show you the most remarkable view in the whole of the Potteries.' He took me up to the top of the Square, past the raggle-taggle shops and tiny, reeking pubs, on to the top of the ridge from which streets led down into the river valley beyond. When we got to this high vantage point, with the three Methodist chapels immediately below us, my father said, 'Behold, The Sytch!'

  There stretched, down and before me, the most striking panorama I had yet seen. The Sytch was the dark heart of the

Potteries, an immense stretch of ground composed in almost equal parts of bare clay earth, black water, mud, industrial detritus both active and abandoned, and fumigerous furnaces, belching forth fire, ashes and smoke. The words 'The Sytch' were spoken in undertones even by hardened Potteries patriots who proudly, as a rule, asserted, 'There's no wealth w'out muck' and, as one of them put it, 'All progress cums fro' sludge.' They knew it was a disgrace, even by Potteries standards. There were houses in it, but no one would admit their address was 'The Sytch'. That was not its official name anyway. There was a river, called the Scotia, which ran through it, probably the most polluted stream in Britain for a century or more, perhaps in the world. Locals called it The Sytch and the name stuck. By 1863 there was The Sytch Croft Coal and Ironstone Works, built by its slimy side. The Sytch was not so much a river as an industrial sewer into which any manufacturer threw or poured or dumped all the waste materials from his establishment. Individuals followed suit: had done for a century.

It was not the only cloaca. The Trent and Mersey canal, gouged out in the 1770s to link the prosperous new large-scale pot-banks of Wedgwood and others to the national communications system, went through the area and received its own contribution of filth. At one time or another a dozen collieries had been set up in The Sytch to mine seams close to the surface. When the easy seams were worked out, they had been abandoned, had flooded and often fallen in, leaving deep cavities which filled with stagnant black water. In addition to potteries, mines and iron furnaces, there were flint grinding mills, an important element in the production of low-cost pots. These filled the sluggish air with dust or covered the ground with muddy slime, according to the season. There was nothing in The Sytch which was not black, dark-grey, deep nigger-brown (as it was then called) or a combination of all three.

The men (and women) who worked there were filthy by the end of the day. 'Poor souls,' my mother often said and sighed. They used to take their midday 'dinner' with them. It was called Lobby and was a thin stew, mainly of potatoes, poured into an ironstone bowl, with a cloth tightly tied round the top. It seemed to me a horrific kind of meal but it was no doubt nourishing and they liked it. All carried their supply of Lobby to work and never thought of eating anything else. There were no canteens. The master potters said, 'Can't afford 'em. Dust want to send us down Carey Street [bankruptcy]?' The colliers were only just getting pit baths by Act of Parliament. Profit margins in pot making were very slender, foreign competition was growing: this elementary economic fact explained all that was wrong with the district, from low wages to pollution.

I don't know who owned The Sytch by the 1930s. The big grandee landlords in North Staffordshire had once been Earl Granville and the Duke of Sutherland (and others), who had dug canals, opened deep pits, founded ironworks and helped to push the railways through. But now the place was a patchwork of freeholds and leaseholds, going cheap. Low-cost firms had moved in, the sort that did not produce well-designed, fine-quality chinaware but coarse dishes and bowls, knobs and weights, number plates and castors, tiles and every kind of china fittings for machines – fuse handles, bits of barometers and thermometers, bathroom fittings. 'Likely us'll make urinals next' was a gloomy saying.

The Sytch was desolation by day for, except when the wind was high, stagnant smoke clouds and a miasma of foetid mist which surged up from its black waters made sure that visibility was low and a semi-darkness prevailed. But at night it came into its own. When my father first showed me The Sytch, dusk was gathering and the place was lighting up. Some of its furnaces were never extinguished. They glowed ominously as the shadows fell and leapt into intense activity as fresh loads of slack coal were thrust through the oven doors. Sparks rocketed fifty feet into the air, huge puffs of livid orange smoke came shooting out of the banks and the countless chimneys, short and tall, which punctuated the horizon every few yards. In the light of the furnace glow, black figures could be seen in frenzied activity, feeding the gluttonous flames with long fire shovels, or raking out the grids beneath, which sent fresh fiery clouds of cinder on to the ground and into the air. Reflected from one cloud to another, the glow reached hundreds – perhaps thousands – of feet into the atmosphere and turned the buildings at the top of Tunstall Square into pink shapes. The dark waters of river, canal and pools doubled the illuminations, and gave to everything a glitter and a mirage of stern beauty. It was not fairyland but devil-land, a desperate romantic hell in which flibbertigibbets and other imps, demons and trolls could dwell in delight.

'Well, and what do you think?' asked my father.

'I love it,' I said. 'It's beautiful and – and – and *wild*.'

'Right, Little Paul. People hate it and want to clean it all away, and they will one day – soon perhaps. But it's the stuff of art and poetry, and we must feast our eyes on it while it lasts. But don't tell your mother what I've said.'

CHAPTER FIVE

The Loop Line

THE BUSINESS OF going to school was the occasion of my first conscious and deliberate act of rebellion. My family were divided. My sisters wanted me to come with them to Stoke to attend the junior department of St Dominic's High School for Girls, where a few boys up to the age of eight were 'received'. My parents really liked this idea too. But my father was not sure that in his position, as headmaster of a local school run by the community, it would be right for me to avoid (as it would appear) the local Catholic elementary school. My mother had a different motive for sending me there: the headmaster was a worthy and good man, Mr Joyce, from Ireland, whose wife, Mrs Joyce, came from a farm in Kerry and had never felt at home in England. She had what the Irish call 'a long, weak family' (i.e. many and small): Thomas, the most serious and responsible; Patrick Joseph, cunning; Brian, wild; Eileen, mystic and poetic; and Sean, tiny. None was over eight. Mrs Joyce, though with the prettiest face in the world, had become fat and inactive, tearful and helpless. My mother befriended and advised her. Mr Joyce was taciturn, withdrawn and seemingly defeatist about the wailings and uproar that surrounded him. My mother's strong sense of propriety and order was offended by the fecklessness and prodigality she observed, so that often 'there is not a penny in the house'. But she recognised in them the true Irish spirit of friendliness and generosity, and felt that for me to bypass Mr Joyce's school might be seen as an affront.

But these considerations did not influence me. I had heard all about St Dominic's from my sisters and wanted to join the intense and exciting life there. It so happened that I read, or had read to me, a tale called 'The Fifth Form at St Dominic's' in a volume called *Chums*, an annual which had reached me second-hand. That, to be sure, was a boy's school and some of the events there alarmed as well as thrilled me; but the coincidence of names was important. Moreover, I did not like the school to which I was condemned. I had seen it. More important, I had heard and smelt it. Taken past its playground by my mother, I had seen a multitude of children, all much bigger than me, pour into this railed enclosure, screaming at the tops of their voices, and wafting towards me a strong whiff of boy stink. I had no wish to be a part and (I feared) victim of that odiferous pandemonium. I made my apprehensions clear; and, when they were nervously ignored by my mother, who deposited me at the school one Monday morning, I protested in the only way that occurred to me. I dodged out of the class at the first opportunity, went out of the school by the gate into the street and made my way home. My mother was not, I could see, wholly surprised, though horrified I had walked through Tunstall by myself. Mutual tears were shed in copious quantities and, by the time my father returned that day, her mind was made up and my future secured. I was not yet five, and had learned that determination and action paid.

Then began a time of adventure. Stoke was at the other end of the Potteries and a journey by rail necessary. The 1930s was the tail-end of the great age of rail in England and we were the beneficiaries of the densest rail network in the world. Until a few years before (1929), the network was still being extended and new lines of track and stations opened. When the early railway barons were driving their arterial routes north, they ignored most of the Potteries. Stoke, almost by chance, was not only made a stop on the main line north, but chosen to be the headquarters of the North Staffordshire Railway. That one event ensured its future status as head of the Six Towns. A large station was built (1848) in Jacobethan Gothick, a luxury hotel, the North Stafford, set up opposite and in the square thus formed a statue of Josiah Wedgwood was duly set up. The only real connection between the main line and the Potteries was a little station at Longport, an insignificant place whose sole purpose was to sustain this connection.

However, in the 1860s and 1870s, as the Potteries expanded, it was swept into the railway age, especially in the form of what were called mineral lines, built to transport heavy goods like coal and clay, not people. One went from the main line at Etruria, whence Wedgwood goods travelled to London, to the Shelton Colliery at Hanley. Another went from Etruria to a colliery in Burslem. A third passed from Longport through The Sytch, Tunstall and on to the big Chatterley-Whitfield colliery. It had branch lines too. This was the railway for which Mr Williams, 'the Master', worked. These little lines, each with its own engines, staff, uniforms and ethos, criss-crossed our region like veins, full of life and peculiarities, run by real experts who never did anything else in their entire lives.

However, the glory of the Potteries was the Loop Line, built in the 1870s when the rail barons realised they were missing a lot of trade. It started at little Longport, worked its way through Tunstall, Burslem, Cobridge (Arnold Bennett's station) and Hanley to end up at Stoke and the main line.

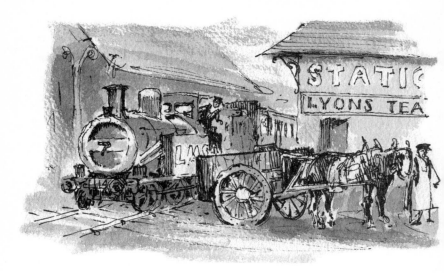

Loop Line station

(There were one or two other obscure stations which do not concern us.) It was like a toy railway. The stations were all complete with goods and parcels offices, stationmaster (wearing a bowler hat at minor stations, a top hat at Stoke), ticket office, porters, waiting rooms and trolleys for putting milk churns on. There were proper signals and points. No expresses ever came through and the engines – *King Edward VII*, the *Duke of Connaught*, the *Princess Royal*, the *Duke of Cambridge* et al – tended to be a generation out of date. All the same, it was a busy and efficient public service. The trains kept perfect time and no accidents were ever recorded. At its peak the Loop Line ran seventy trains a day, one every fifteen minutes.

My sisters and I loved this railway. It was 'ours'. And it was part of the great London, Midland and Scottish Railway, largest of the Big Four – nicest, too, we thought. People were very attached to leading institutions then. It was a form of patriotism. You were either Oxford or Cambridge, Eton or

Harrow, Yorkshire or Lancashire, Gentlemen or Players, whether or not you had connections with any. North Staffs despised South Staffs — it was 'stuck up'. The Potteries despised the rest of North Staffs as 'idle'. Potteries people particularly disliked Newcastle-under-Lyme, which was older, had no pot-banks and 'did nothing'. It was 'stuck up' too. Of the railways, the LNER was 'common', the Southern 'boring' and the Great Western was yet another 'stuck-up' institution. The LMS was 'just right'; its maroon colours were ours.

You went down a steep track to get into Tunstall Station, a cavernous place under a bridge, of smoke-stained dingy brick, dark and fumigerous. I loved the powerful stamp machine which put the date on our cardboard tickets with a loud 'thoomp'. Stationmaster Greatbatch was in charge, assisted by Porter Hamps, who waved the green flag when it was time for the train to go. Mr Greatbatch sometimes saw us into our carriage and made sure the heavy brass door handle was securely shut. The dignity with which he took out his huge steel watch — a 'turnip' I was told, to my mystification — consulted it, then nodded gravely to Mr Hamps, was an exercise in the courtly manners which antedated rail and went back to the stagecoaches.

The train would always whistle loudly when it left Tunstall, run fast down the slope which led into The Sytch (or the edge of it), then chuff and pant laboriously up the hill to Burslem. We often had the carriage to ourselves and if we did we would defend the door to prevent 'rough Burslem boys', on their way to Hanley High School, from getting in. Clare led this operation with great determination and spirit. The boys had to go to another compartment — there were no corridors, of course. I soon knew by heart the pictures under the luggage racks: *Blackpool, North Shore, The Esplanade at Rhyl, Paddle Steamer, Coniston Lake, The Pier, Hoylake*. (This despised and dreary place was where the Stones took their holidays.) They were all brown and flyblown, for the LMS put superannuated coaches on the Loop Line. The seats were of much-worn plush and emitted immense dust clouds when thwacked. It was strictly forbidden for children to get into the luggage racks, so Clare performed this antinomian gesture as a daily ritual, hoisting herself up in one lithe movement, a feat of athleticism in which she took pride and delight. Her other trick was to swing herself from one rack to the other.

At Cobridge, where no one ever got on or off — it was a mere platform — a curious thing happened. The driver always shut down his engine and, for half a minute, a great silence descended, in which you could hear birds sing. During this time I read over and over again the enamelled iron signs which were joined to the wooden railings: 'Virol: Expectant Mothers Need It'; 'Virol: Growing Lads Need It;' 'Virol: Convalescents Need It'. I studied advertisements intently as soon as I could read. A lot were concerned with energy, or the lack of it. Horlicks ran a series of fascinating tales, in comic-strip form, about men, women or children who were failing at work, home or school because of a dread complaint called Midnight Starvation. Then a friend told them about Horlicks, the family solemnly quaffed it before going to bed and careers, house-keeping and studies prospered. Even better were the Guinness ads, which then were drawn by a genius who depicted pint glasses of foaming Guinness swallowed by ostriches, and other stupendous events depicting animals stealing the hard-earned porter of red-faced men. (All these ads would now be banned, of course.)

At Hanley there was bustle. Sometimes an elderly gent got in (by elderly I mean anyone over forty). In those days the old liked to converse with children and children liked to be talked to. It would not happen now, but the Thirties was an age of innocence. The man would say, 'Off ter school, thin? Brownhills most likely, ar?'

'No, St Dominic's.'

'Oo aye, that's Roman, ar? Dost learn Latin?'

'A little.'

'Ee, ah wishtad learned Latin, it's a reet sign of knowledge, tha knowst. 'Im as knows Latin is a superior person, they say. Congregations. Irregular verbs, that sort of stuff, eh? Ee, I envy thee. Stick to thy books while thee canst and thee'll not regret it, believe thou me.'

The Potteries people were always gregarious, talkative up to a point: judged everyone as equals (and voted Labour overwhelmingly, even in those days) but never challenged class distinctions based on education. They would address anyone, even the Duke of Sutherland, if they got the chance. But they did not seek to dispossess him of his broad acres; on the contrary, they applauded his decision to throw Trentham Park, his huge, unlived-in palace near Stoke, with magnificent gardens and pavilions, open to the public. They positively liked an aristocracy, in fact, provided it was generous and public-spirited, and they could laugh at it too. The Earl of Derby, who was fat, jovial and pronounced his 'a's short, as they did, was particularly popular, 'allus ready wuv a five-pun note'.

What I liked most about going to school on the Loop Line were those early winter mornings when the carriage windows misted over, providing me with six large virgin surfaces on which to draw with my fingers. This was sheer delight. I quickly discovered that they made a perfect medium for caricatures. The first thing I really studied in the newspapers, both those we got at home and those I saw in the library reading room, were the cartoons. It was a golden age for

The Loop Line

political cartoons, not only because of the ability of the artists, led by the incomparable David Low, my first graphic hero, but because the inter-war years provided a magnificent cast of characters who strutted on the world stage.

I learned to draw Hitler with his quiff, moustache, salute and swastika, and pouchy eyes; Mussolini with his huge chin and forage cap with an eagle on it; Stalin with his handlebar moustache, amazing eyebrows and dark hair crowding his low forehead; Roosevelt with his grin, big chin thrust up, cigarette in a holder clenched between his teeth; and Churchill, with his tiny nose, big cigar and bald head, complete with spotted bow tie, black jacket and waistcoat, and striped pants. I could do Goering too, fat and greedy, with flashy field-marshal's uniform and immense peaked hat, holding his baton. Baldwin's

knobbly face rather defeated me, though he had, like Stalin, a useful pipe. Chamberlain had an umbrella, but his face was too difficult for me to epitomise. I tried very hard to do Lloyd George, with his wild hair and cloak, 'the Goat' or the 'Welsh Wizard'. General Franco, a diminutive man with forage cap and big nose over swarthy chin and moustache, with baggy breeches, was easier, and Chiang Kai-shek was a fairly straight-forward Chinaman in military uniform, the collar buttoned up tightly – he was accompanied by Madame Chiang in female mandarin robes, a trick I got from Strube, the *Express* cartoonist.

Drawing on a misty train window required simplicity and self-confidence, so I tended to stick to the ones I knew I could do, headed by Hitler, Musso and Stalin. One morning I had just completed them and was having a go at Churchill (not in office then but prominent and known to all), when a silver-haired gent got in at Hanley and surveyed my work with some surprise, which turned to delight when he saw Churchill emerge. 'Well,' said he. 'Well, well, well. God bless my soul, young fellow, and how old are you? Five, eh? Well, well, well. You'll go far, boy, I predict it. Dictators, eh? You know how to do them, by heaven! And Winston too! I would he were at the helm of state now. Bow tie, cigar – you've got it all! Ha! Ha!' This Dickensian performance, not uncommon in those days, when eccentrics and characters abounded, and men spoke exactly what they thought in the way that suited them, was followed by much fumbling in the fobs of his waistcoat and finally a note of triumph: 'Ah-ha! What have we here? A silver coin of the realm! Here, boy, take this sixpence and buy yourself some nice, good pencils. Tell your mother it is a little gift of appreciation from an old gentleman who admires talent. Ha, ha, ha!'

My sisters demurred, but he insisted and the matter was reported back to my mother, who agreed the coin should be retained but given to the Little Sisters of Mercy, currently her favourite order of nuns. My father, when he got to hear about it, pronounced it unjust. 'Why, it's the boy's first earnings!' So he gave me a sixpence from his own pocket. What he did not know was that my mother's favourite brother, my Uncle Jimmy, had already given me a sixpence on a 'flying visit' in his new Wolseley Tourer, and she thought two sixpences at a time might give me 'wrong ideas' and I would end up being 'marred'. So I had a shilling and, after much thought, bought a box of paints, my first.

Stoke Station, our terminus, was huge, with a glass roof, a bridge over the rails and, wonderful, an underground passage, which we used every evening to reach the platform where our return train waited. There were machines too: a fascinating one with a huge alphabetical wheel which, in return for a penny, punched your name in relief on a strip of aluminium that could then be attached to your pencil box (mine, with three long compartments revolving round an axis at one end, was a new and precious possession). Another tested your grip, health, registered your height and weight, and told your fortune.

A third was tempting but false. It held a great many desirable small toys in its big glass top, together with vast numbers of jelly beans. It had a silver crane which, when a penny was inserted, became active and could be directed by a lever to the toy you particularly wanted. The crane was a mechanical grab, which lowered itself on to the toy, then contracted its fingers round it, lifting it up and some jelly beans too. But the fingers were maddeningly feeble. Long before the grab had steered itself towards the hole out of the machine it was sure to have let the toy slip out of its dithering grasp and all you ever got were a few miserable beans – sweets held in low repute anyway (this was half a century before President Reagan made them popular). No one was ever known to get a toy out of this beastly machine. My brother Tom claimed that a similar one, on Hanley Station, yielded its treasure to a series of well-aimed kicks at its base. But no amount of kicking by Clare and me had any effect on the Stoke one. So we left it severely alone: my first lesson in the fraudulence of the world and the need for restraint in facing its lures.

When we had been going for a month on our six-days-a-week journeys (for in those days we all went to school on Saturday morning, just as the grown-ups worked until midday), a notable event took place. Everything about the train seemed huge to me: the height of the carriage, the size of the engine, its pistons, wheels, funnel, buffers, fender and cylinders, the doors, the distance from the step outside it to the ground and even to the platform. Clare and Elfride got out first when we reached Stoke, and the train hissed to a halt. I appeared in the doorway, satchel on my back, and Clare would then swing me high in the air and deposit me on the platform. I liked this, but I also liked to get out by myself, which was perfectly easy at Tunstall, on our way home.

One morning Clare was a little slow at turning to get me: she had plants she was taking to show the botany mistress. I stepped down and vanished into the depth between platform and train. It was dark and dim there, with only an oblong of light above my head. The wheels of the train seemed enormous, smelt strongly of oil and shuddered, as if anxious to spring into motion again. Clare's voice came from a long distance: 'Where's Paul?' and I replied, 'I'm down here.' She said, later, that my voice sounded 'very tiny' and 'forlorn'. Concerned, frightened faces peered down at me, there was a hullabaloo as porters were summoned. The stoker from the train jumped down and lifted me up, and strong arms deposited me on the platform. It was all over in seconds and I was not really frightened at all, except at the prospect of being blamed for causing trouble. A crowd had collected, as crowds did in those days at the smallest incident, many people having nothing to do – unemployed, I suppose. And Potteries people all believed they were born with a right to comment. 'The little lad might've been squashed reet flat.' 'Ar, or brok 'is bones.' 'Dangerous them holes betwixt train an' platform. Ah say this is too wide, like.' 'It's allus been like that at Stoke. Think 'or old folk, an all'.

Then there was a sudden deferential parting and Mr Oldcastle, the stationmaster, having donned his top hat for the occasion, strode on to the scene. He lifted his topper, though whether to me, my sisters, or the crowd I do not know, and said, 'This will have to be reported to Higher Authority. I will undertake to do so. There may be a Hazard. On the other hand there may have been carelessness. Or both. The young lad is unharmed, is he? Good. Take additional care next time, boy.' Then, suddenly reaching a decision, 'Tell Mrs Silverbright in Refreshments to give the boy a glass of that special Sarsparilla to set him up. And now' – consulting his enormous turnip – 'the service must be resumed.'

That was the one time I had dealings with Mr Oldcastle, who normally appeared only when the Euston Express to Glasgow stopped, to deposit the Duke of Sutherland or Earl Granville on the platform. Clare was subdued, thinking what my mother might say when the incident was reported to her. Then Elfride, who was not without a certain legitimate guile, said, 'The stationmaster said there might be a hazard and we should make a point of repeating that to Mum.' And so they did, and my mother's account of the episode to neighbours and relatives revolved around the word 'hazard' or, as she put it, 'the perils of that dreadful, filthy station'. However, she was no fool. After publicly praising my courage in misadventure and the fact that I had not cried, she said to me privately, 'You have a disconcerting habit of drawing attention to yourself.'

St Dominic's was a kind of paradise to me for a variety of reasons. First it was high up on the top of Hartshill, outside Stoke – higher up even than Priory House, which was attached to it. It was a white, two-storey building, formerly the Regency home of a rich family, with splendid gardens and grounds, converted into playing fields. One of these grassy enclosures was said to be 'a whole acre in extent'. The school was spotlessly clean, polished and scrubbed, as all institutions run by nuns were. All was neat and orderly, quiet and polite.

The nuns were delightful creatures in their black-and-white habits, voluminous, starched, crackling and swishing, with rosary beads rattling – all reassuring noises to me. They smelt of soap and fresh linen. Sister Angela, in whose care I was placed, was true to her name, angelic, gave me hugs and kisses, and would put me on her knee if she thought I looked homesick. I could, in fact, already read, but she quickly taught me to write in neat, elegant letters, a skill in which Dominicans are always expert.

There were several boys of roughly my age, like me in short grey woollen trousers and jackets. I had a grey cap, with the special black-and-white cross of St Dominic embroidered on it. I had grey turnover stockings and black, shiny, lace-up shoes. My satchel was brown leather, with three compartments, all buckle-shut. This was undoubtedly progress. Even more impressive, I had a desk to myself, or rather a little table, with chair to match. After a week with pencil, I was 'promoted to ink' and began the mysteries of nib, pen, blotter and writing with a medium that smudged.

I was left-handed. My parents discovered this early in my existence and made no attempt, as most parents of left-handers by nature then did, to force me into right-handedness. My mother said, 'The Duke of York is like you. His Majesty, King George V, forced him to write with his right hand, so he could shoot properly, and as a result the poor Duke contracted a stammer. So your father and I think you should be allowed to do things with your left hand if you find it easier.'

My father said, 'Leonardo da Vinci was left-handed. So was Michelangelo, so you're in good company, Little Paul.'

However, writing with ink was not easy for me. Holding the pen in the usual way, but in the left hand, meant you smudged all you wrote and I quickly learned, with Sister

Angela's guidance, to curl my hand above and round the pen, and so avoid the ink: a practice which looks (but is not) awkward and attracts comment even to this day, but got me through the age of ink — now happily buried. Sister Angela taught me how to draw little devotional diagrams of the Sacred Heart, the Virgin Mary, the Crucifixion and the Nativity, and to colour them with crayons. She had an innocent, childlike mind, full of religious images, and she delighted to tell me stories of the saints and martyrs: how St Stephen was stoned to death, St Peter crucified upside down, St Sebastian shot to death with arrows, St Bartholomew had his skin torn off, St Catherine sentenced to the wheel and so forth. These atrocities mingled with the story of St Ignatius of Loyola, the Jesuit soldier, and St Dominic preaching, St Francis talking to the birds and St Theresa having her heart pierced with the arrows of God's love. I particularly liked the story of Jesus getting lost in Jerusalem and being found arguing with the elders in the Temple. I could see myself in that role.

Sister Angela was young, pretty and sentimental, and incapable of anger, censure or criticism. She radiated a simple love which found its way to my heart. Sister Veronica, who taught me 'sums', was older and capable of severity, though she too liked to hug me and occasionally bestow a kiss. She also said things which made me think. 'Mathematics, Paul, are distasteful to most people, though a few find them the elixir of life, by which I mean a delicious kind of drink. You don't like maths because you are an artist. So I say: learn enough maths, now and later, to satisfy the authorities. It is worth it because when you finally pass your School Certificate in compulsory maths, you need never think of maths ever again. That is the secret of life. What you have to do, *do* — at all costs. Then forget all about it. If you don't do it, they will be at you for ever.' This was the first piece of serious advice I received from anyone apart from my family; it proved to be good advice and, on the whole, I have followed it.

The mistress in charge of the Junior School was Sister Regina, a 'very senior nun indeed', said to be 'a terror'. She was tall and walked in a slow and stately manner, whereas junior nuns bustled. She dwelt in a room by herself and administered things. She spoke precisely, with emphasis on certain words and syllables. 'Girls [she ignored boys as non-existent], remember that young ladies do not *squeal* or *snigger* or laugh in an in*dec*orous way. *Mod*ulate your tones. R*estrain* your voices. Make your movements *grace*ful. And what do I wish *not* to hear?' The girls chorused, 'Talking in the corridors, Sister Regina.'

There were many small rules but few punishments, save the shame of a public rebuke. Sister Angela could not rebuke, as she was sure to cry in doing so. Sister Veronica could, but seldom did, preferring to persuade. Sister Regina could rebuke: 'Young lady, I am pro*found*ly disappointed in you.' Or even: 'You are a *wretch*.' The most serious punishment of all was being sent to sit in the deckchair in Sister Regina's room for an unspecified period. How the deckchair had originally got there was lost in the mists of time. By accident, it had become a punishment stool, a throne of dread, so that the threat 'Do you really wish to be sent to the DECKCHAIR, you naughty girl/boy in Sister Regina's PRIVATE ROOM?' was a terrible thing to hear. I was never subjected to this ultimate sanction but I grasped how effective it was and have never since looked kindly at those awkward and dangerous pieces of furniture.

My aim in those days was to have a busy desk. I looked with envy at my elders in the big junior schoolroom, whose tables were littered with exercise books, textbooks and dictionaries. All I had on mine was one book for reading, one exercise book for writing in and rarely both together. Never were there three things on my desk, the minimum to make it look important. This longing was strong with me and I did not know how to satisfy it. With this exception my days in the junior school were happy and profitable. I was soon reading and writing with proficiency. We did little plays, mainly of an uplifting nature. I was by turns St Joseph, St Christopher and Remus, a co-founder of Rome.

I loved the gymnasium. The great Miss King, of whom I had heard much before joining the school, singled me out for friendship as the younger brother of Clare, her favourite pupil. She taught me to run properly and to do the high jump. She was a striking figure in her black gymslip with a micro-skirt, her long shapely legs in black lisle stockings, her beautifully pipe-clayed white pumps and her straight black hair, brushed until it shone and neatly displayed in a page-boy cut. She looked like a Principal Boy in a pantomime, youthful, immensely alert and vigorous, brave and dashing. 'Come along, girls,' she would say. 'You can do it, you must do it. You *will* do it.' She could do cartwheels and amazing handsprings, back-springs and standing jumps. She said she would teach me to box but that the nuns would not let her. She said, 'Paul, you must learn how to box. It is essential for a boy to defend himself scientifically. One, two, down go the bad boys! You must do boxing the moment you go to the boys' school. Better to have learned before, though. I will see what I can do, secretly. In the meantime, do press-ups' – and she had me doing them until I was dizzy. I loved Sister Angela, but I worshipped Miss King. She never sat me on her knee. On the contrary, it was 'Let's go for a run in Break'. And we did, me panting to keep up with the masterful figure. Clare reported, 'Miss King says you are a Brick.'

There were not many other boys and none of them interested
me much. Leo Goldenhill was the son of a coal manager in
Shelton and his claim to celebrity was that he had been allowed
once to fire his father's shotgun. But Miss King said he was
'wet', a term just coming into vogue. He kept horrid lumps
of plasticine in his trouser pockets and smelt of it. Kenneth
Ternihough, son of a chemist, played the recorder a bit but was
snivelly and tearful over his work, an only child. Then there were
the Botteslow twins, Arthur and Emily, who came from a farm
in Trent Vale and claimed to have a pet fox, which the nuns
forbade them to bring to school 'under any circumstances', as
Sister Veronica put it – a puzzling line as my mother said that
Councillor Boothen, who occasionally came to see my father,
was too 'circumstantial'. The twins smelt of their fox a bit, or
Arthur did. He said little but had a bad word, 'ruddy'.

Of the girls, my favourite was Rolanda, a pink-faced child
whose blonde hair was pulled into a tail, unusual then, and
who often gave me a kiss when no one was looking. My
enemy was Rena Milton, whose family was rich and who
wore (after a battle with the nuns) a coral necklace with a
small gold cross attached. She was quite fierce, violet-eyed,
with black curly hair and red shiny cheeks. She offered to
box me and give me what she called 'a few good thumps'.
She was clever and always anxious to outsmart me and
others. Miss King called her 'Miss Minx' and prophesied
'trouble to come'. Rena boasted of grand goings-on at
home, being allowed to attend 'dinner parties', not just high
teas, of visits to the theatre in Manchester and putting on
scent, which she called 'perfume'. She referred to me as
'spotty-face' because of my freckles. She never cried but
could make other girls cry. She knew the inside of Sister
Regina's private room well and what it was like to be
sentenced to the deckchair.

✳

Much of our time was spent preparing to make our First Communions, which in my case took place when I was six. Sister Angela explained patiently to us the difference between Transubstantiation and Consubstantiation, which we did not take in; but we thoroughly understood that Jesus actually came into our mouths in the form of the holy wafer and that our tummies had to be properly prepared to receive him by fasting from midnight and by *confessing our sins*. This was, potentially, an alarming experience since it meant going into a dark box, drawing the velvet curtain, then speaking to the priest through a grille. Sister Angela rehearsed this with us in the big church, just behind Priory House (now unoccupied). I did not mind confessing to Sister Angela but was less sure about talking in the dark to an unknown priest.

Moreover, what to confess? Sister Angela said that bad things done before our fifth birthday did not count. Nor did mere school transgressions, like making a noise in the refectory or running down a corridor. Lies and stealing counted as sins. So did 'disobedience to a lawful command'. Sister Angela did not help as she kept saying, 'I can't think you have committed any *real* sins.' But not to have anything to confess defeated the whole object of the sacrament of penance and might, so Sister Veronica thought, be construed as 'spiritual pride'. Besides, it might seem 'wet', to use Miss King's word. She, consulted, thought I should confess 'getting your own way more often than you ought', so I put that down for one. Saying the word 'ruddy' counted for another. My mother, to whom I confided my worries about not having enough to confess, laughed and said, 'Don't cross your bridges until you come to them.' She also pointed out that I had once told, not indeed a lie, but a 'fib', and although this was some time before and fell outside the ecclesiastical statute of limitations, it made three sins of a sort, and both my mother and Sister Angela pronounced three 'quite enough'.

So I made my first Confession in a little voice – the same I used when I fell down on to the track at Stoke Station – and the priest said irritably, 'Speak up, child, you're a little hard to hear' and I doubt if he understood a word of my mumble, but he pronounced absolution and said, 'Tell the next to make it snappy.' This, when related, made my mother laugh again and say, 'He's been seeing gangster films.'

Immediately we came out of the church, Rena Milton pounced on me: 'Well, smutty-face, and how many sins did *you* confess?'

I said, 'Three.'

She positively smirked and, putting a hand on her hip and twirling, said, 'I had *nine!*'

I felt defeated but when I told Sister Angela about it, she looked shocked and said, 'She has broken the Seal of the Confession.' This confused me greatly, for the only seal I could think of balanced a big rubber ball on its nose or, in the Guinness advertisement, a full pint of stout.

The next week we made our First Communion, again in the big church. The girls were decked out in white – dress, socks, shoes, hair ribbons, gloves – and carried new shiny white prayer books. We had new grey suits, white shirts and red ties ('red for the blood Jesus shed for us,' said Sister Angela). Our prayer books were black. We were particularly told not to chew the Host but to let it melt in our mouths and swallow it. I glanced at Rena and she was *chewing*, quite unashamedly and, when she had finished, stuck out her tongue at me as far as it would stretch, to prove her point.

The Communion, attended by parents in their glory and pride, was followed by a sumptuous state breakfast in the main refectory of the convent. This palatial edifice, by the

great Catholic architect Joseph Hansom, I then believed to be
the largest building in the world and this was the first time I
had been in it. The great thing about Catholic institutions –
and even monastic orders and the like, be they Jesuits or
Dominicans or Franciscans, the last two of which take vows
of poverty – is that when they feast they truly feast and the
meal is not merely splendid but splendidly presented. It was
my introduction to the idea of a feast, and I loved every
second and aspect of it: the room, decorated with boughs and
sprigs of spring leaves; the table, immensely long, with
spotless crackling linen cloths and napkins folded into mitres,
and with pots and vases of flowers along its entire length,
producing great flashes of colour; there were silver spoons
and forks, and silver vessels or trophies placed at intervals.
The nuns moved about, fussing and carrying plates, for they
did not feast themselves.

The food was delicious: not merely bacon, eggs and
sausages (something we never had in triplicate at home – only
two of the three at once), but *hot rolls*, a new delicacy to me.
Moreover, as a supreme luxury the meal began with grapefruit, cut into halves, sugared and with a crystallised cherry in
the middle. This was a Babylonian touch and a complete
novelty, for grapefruit had only just 'come in' (as my mother
put it) and none of us had had one before. Grapefruit,
indeed, were one of the choicest novelties of the Thirties. We
knew of them, if at all, only from movie stories or reports of
them. Jimmy Cagney, in an early gangster epic, told his
yapping moll, 'Aw, shut up!' and pushed a half-grapefruit in
her face. Ash-blonde Agnes in *The Big Sleep*, presiding over the
sinister bookshop, was asked by Marlow if it sold books and
snarled, 'Wadya think these are, grapefruit?' In short,
grapefruit were the latest thing and it was highly fashionable
of the nuns to provide them.

The Dominican nuns ate little themselves but they delighted in feeding us well. Almost on the first day they introduced me to a new pudding, 'Floating Islands', pieces of sponge cake with a white-of-egg topping, surrounded by a sea of custard. They had a delicious version of Spotted Dog, known as 'Reverend Mother's Leg' to the girls, who rather shocked me by the unceremonious manner with which they treated the holy ladies. I found schoolgirls very critical, much more so than boys, who tended to accept anything that happened stoically.

I made friends with a girl called Vanya, of foreign origin, I think — perhaps from Malta — who, though exactly my age, seemed much older and knew about things I was unaware existed: that the best clothes for females (a new word to me), were made in Paris and were *horribly expensive* (her mother's phrase). They were called *modes*. When we drew together, she pointed out not only that women were shorter than men — I had noticed that myself — but that they had quite different figures. She taught me to draw narrow waists, wider hips and sticking-out busts for women, as well as longer hair. She showed me how to draw a bun, with a hat on it. It was one of my most rooted characteristics as an artist that I always began a figure with the feet. My mother thought this extraordinary and laughed a lot. My father said that, granted the angle of vision of a small boy, it was natural, though he confessed it was rare. Vanya showed me how to draw a woman's feet, with pointed toes and high heels. My mother shook her head a little sadly when I showed her my first drawing of a 'proper woman'. She said, almost to herself, 'Oh, it's always a piercing moment when you realise a growing child is getting information from sources other than its family. It's the first sign of loss of control.' She hugged me close, as though I was going to walk out of the door and never come back.

I was invited to tea at Vanya's house and met her mother: slight, dark of skin with flashing brown eyes, well-dressed. My mother asked if she wore lipstick but I could not tell. They had a parlourmaid, Flossie, who came at the summons of a little silver bell. Flossie brought excellent sandwiches, sliced very thin and containing ingredients new to me: potted shrimps, anchovies and, amazingly, lobster mayonnaise. I knew this last item was what my father called 'Babylonian luxury' and my mother was quite shocked to hear I was given such 'unsuitable food'.

We come now to the important matter of children's sandwiches. What a child's mother put into his or her sandwiches was noticed and commented on in the Potteries. I heard the phrase 'She's a poor sandwich woman' used by a critical mother. Or: 'She's a jam sandwich woman.' Jam was regarded as the lowest or meanest possible filling for a sandwich; little better than just butter. ('Bread and marge' was worse still, but I never knew of a case.) Personally, I was quite happy with a jam filling; what I despised was just lettuce, without even any tomato, let alone cheese. Favourites were: corned beef with chutney; roast beef with all the fat cut off and gherkins; tinned salmon (fresh was unheard of) with slices of cucumber and mayonnaise; and Gentlemen's Relish, from a beautiful flat white jar brought to my mother periodically by her favourite cousin, my Uncle Jack. I abominated cold pork or mutton, rhubarb jam and anything involving beetroot.

There was a universal convention, observed even in Vanya's home (which otherwise, my mother said, 'appears to be dangerously extravagant') that at children's tea parties sandwiches were always served first 'to take the edge off hunger', and not until the sandwich plates had been cleared were you allowed to 'go on' to the trifles, blancmanges, custards, biscuits, jellies and cakes, though these dainties were already spread out on the table and gloriously inviting. 'If you don't eat sandwiches first,' my mother said, 'you are tempted to eat too much of the rich things and become sick.' I did not agree with this, as a cold mutton sandwich was more likely to make me sick than anything else; and you were made to eat your share of whatever sandwiches were on offer by public opinion — for if you hesitated, the other children would accuse you of holding up the progress of the party. But that was the rule, so sandwiches we ate.

Then came the advent of Peter Hennessy. He was a small, wiry, joyful boy, a little older than me and much more freckled, with wild hair and huge eyes, fiendishly active, with devastating high spirits, always laughing and doing. Sister Angela was a bit alarmed by him but Sister Veronica doted on Peter, especially after she discovered he was a mathematical 'genius', and he got a lot of her rare kisses. Peter liked everyone to be happy and so did his mother. When I first went to tea there, with Vanya and the horrid Rena (whom Peter fancied from the start), I was overwhelmed by Mrs Hennessy's friendliness and fun and, still more, the amazing spread on the tea table. Every variety of trifle was there, three jellies of different colours, including blue (a rarity), a nut blancmange (ditto) and cakes of the nicest kind — Fuller's Walnut, a Battenberg, chocolate éclairs, Eccles Cakes, Newcastle Crumbles, a French apple tart (a novelty to me) and a rich fruit cake known as Children's Wedding Cake which, when described to my mother, she pronounced 'downright wicked'. But there were no sandwiches — none at all. I enquired why not. Mrs Hennessy was surprised. 'Sandwiches? Why eat sandwiches at a birthday tea when there's plenty of cake. But we can make you some if you want.' I hastily explained the rule and she laughed until her dangly earrings shook (she was a little, gay woman, a *jolie laide*, festooned in exotic jewellery, like a whizzing, sparkling insect). 'Well,' she said. 'What a silly rule. There are no rules here. You eat what you want. And everything you want. Or nothing at all — like me! This is Liberty Hall!'

I rather envied Peter his Liberty Hall. But when I described it to my mother she made one of her disapproving faces and said, 'Licence Hall, more likely. Mark my words!' But when she actually met Mrs Hennessy she took to her immediately, as often happened: what she rejected in theory she relished in practice. She even said, 'Mona Hennessy is a zippy little thing,' a rare use of current slang. They met for coffee and became friends. And I liked Peter. He was always in trouble and I sensed, though I did not of course know the phrase, that he was mad, bad and dangerous to know. But he was exciting. Things happened when he was there. It was a dash of pepper in the calm, loving, idyllic existence of St Dominic's junior school.

There were, however, ominous hints that the idyll would end. Even Sister Angela admitted, 'Now you are seven you will soon have to leave and go to St Joseph's.' She shook her head sadly.

'Is St Joseph's horrid, Sister?' She shook her head even more sadly. St Joseph's was a brand-new school up the road from St Dominic's, run by the Christian Brothers. They were a fierce Irish order of schoolmasters, very successful at turning clever boys into brilliant scholars and taming wild boys by relentless corporal punishment.

Peter Hennessy said, 'My mum says they are savages and she won't let me near them.' All this was bad news for me.

Vanya said, 'Please don't leave me,' as if I had any choice in the matter. She offered to say three Hail Marys every day to prevent it happening.

Rena at first laughed and said, 'Those Christian Brothers

will beat you every day with their straps, my father says.' But later, she too cried. All depended on my father, however, and I was becoming closer to him.

Chapter Six
Smoke into Art

WE WERE SKETCHING the church at Audley, just west of Tunstall, sitting side by side on the wall. It was one of my father's favourite churches and he drew it again and again, from different angles. He was teaching me about shade and shadow. Then he said, 'Tomorrow I'll show you Burslem.' That was where he worked, where his Art School was; but he had never taken me there. So I was excited.

My mother said, 'You'll come back covered in smuts. No one goes to Burslem unless they have to.' Then, to my father: 'Don't let him fall into the clay bin.' This was a new idea to me. What was a clay bin? Why must I not fall into it?

We went by bicycle. My father loved his bike. It was a Raleigh; 'The best bike in the world,' he said. 'It keeps me fit. Exercises the lungs. Tightens my stomach muscles and stops me getting fat. I'd be a dead man except for my bike. This Raleigh is the Poor Man's Rolls-Royce, the Rich Man's Guide to Longevity, the gymnasium of the Middle Classes.' He was given to such rhetoric when he was happy. 'Now, Little Paul, let's off to Burslem, Onlie Begetter of the Pot-Bank, the Florence of Porcelain, the home of smoke and smuts!' My small bike was not as fast as his, but he liked to go slowly, looking at the buildings, commenting, enthusing. We went

down King William Street, past the Methodist skeleton
chapel — 'No progress on St Chad's, I see, and no matter
either, a poor design and worse execution.' Then across the
railway lines and up the hill to Burslem, making our way
through a maze of industrial activity. This was The Sytch
Road, by rights Scotia Road, but nobody called it that. 'Don't
worry about The Sytch. It's an eyesore, true, but without that
Lake of Tears people would be much poorer. Dirt generates
wealth, Little Paul, remember that. They say there's no smoke
without fire. I say there's no silver without smoke.' We paused
and got off our bikes outside a big black building which he
called 'the new town hall, a brute'. Behind us was a big works.
'That's a print shop. Good jobs going there, every autumn. I
like to get my boys and girls places in printing. There's more
money in that than in pots. But less art.'

He took me into the Market Place and showed me the Old
Town Hall. 'Now there is a splendid piece of work. Robinson
built it in 1850, so it's got four generations of smoke ingrained
into it. It's as black as my hat' (his hat was, in fact, brown and
worn with brim down, artist-style, cocked over one eye). This
Old Town Hall, still standing I am glad to say, he drew often,
with its giant pilasters, huge portico with a flashy baroque
top, massive pillars on either side. 'It's a very confident building, Little Paul, and confidence is everything in art. Because
when you are confident you can dash at it! Now, look at the
places that generate the money to build town halls and everything else!' I looked and there in the very heart of Burslem
were the pot-banks, dozens of them, puffing smoke and flame.
There is a photograph, taken from the air at just about this
time in the mid-1930s, which shows the pottery firms clustered
about the Old Town Hall, nine of them within a stone's throw,
each with its family of bottle-shaped ovens.

There was, indeed, something human and familiar about

Burslem's Old Town Hall

these pot-banks. My father explained that potting in Burslem went back to the thirteenth century at the time of the Crusades. A farmer discovered good china clay on his land and started to make pots. His daughters learned how to turn them on a wheel and he built an oven to fire them. Other farmers followed suit. All pot-banks started as farms and were built in the farmyard, square-shaped. There was an entrance gate where the carts came in, a space in the middle of the square where they were loaded and buildings all round. 'In fact,' said my father, 'it's just occurred to me that pot-banks are rather like Oxford and Cambridge colleges, as you'll see for yourself when you go there. They each started with one courtyard of buildings, with a porter's lodge opening on to the street. Then, when they expanded, they built another court-yard and so on. In pot-banks those courtyards are called squares. They started out with the original square, where they did everything. Then they gradually added specialist squares. You take the Garrett Works now. The original square is still there, with its porter's lodge. No one can get in without reporting to the lodge – just like Cambridge. Now there's a Dishmaker's Square, a Plate Square, a Saucer Square, a Coloured Body Square and a Printer's Square. It has seven biscuit ovens, fourteen glaze ovens and sixteen kilns for enamelling.'

We went into the Royal Pottery just off the Market Square. My father was well known there – indeed, he was a familiar figure at all the works. He introduced me to Jacob Thrower, one of the foremen, who showed me round a bottle-shaped oven, now cool. 'This 'un are forty foot 'igh, medium like. See tha top – that's t'hovel. Them door on t'shoulder is for inspection – go up 'a on ladder. And them rods is damper chains fer pullin' out doors fer draught. Dost understand, lad? Look 'e 'ere.' He pointed to a tiny hole in the base of the bottle oven. 'This 'un is sight 'ole. Thou can see inside when it's firing.'

In this oven the unfired pots, piled in great earthenware cases called saggars, were already being stacked. 'It's firing tonight, dost see?' The furnace was at the side, a truckful of coal ready. 'Im there, 'e's the Gloss Fireman. 'Ow do, Percy?' One of the customs I noted about the Potteries was how many of the potters had Christian names taken from the surnames of the great medieval families of the North and north Midlands, not only Percys but Howards and Stanleys, Cliffords and Cecils, Staffords and Nevilles, Talbots, Russells and Montagues. These given names commemorated family traditions of children born 'the wrong side of the blanket', an expression of Mrs Williams, which puzzled me.

Jacob told me about his surname, 'Thrower. That's a real Potteries name, dost tha' know? It's a trade, 'ere. A thrower dos cast clay fer pots. In this works there's twenty-eight trades. There's scourers and handlers, placers and throwers, turners and slipmakers, pressers and runners. An' ah' doan't know what. It's a grand trade, potting, but there's nowt much money in't.' He broke into song:

> Colliery lads make gold and silver
> Pottery lads make brass.
> 'Oor would marry a Buslem [Burslem] thrower
> When there's plenty of colliery lads?

'They sing that in Manchester,' said my father, laughing. 'But they say "factory" instead of "pottery", and "handloom weaver" for "Burslem thrower".'

'Aye,' said Jacob Thrower, 'but catch me down in t'mine, nah! Ah remember the big fall at Herbert Deep Number Two. Fifty men went in, five came out. Aye! They call it the Widow Maker, that bloody pit – beg your pardon, Mr Johnson.'

This pot-bank, like all of them, throbbed with life. Each employed dozens of women, sometimes scores, to do the jobs requiring delicacy of touch: working the clay on the wheels, sculpting the fancy bits, above all painting the patterns on the china. It was the hand-painted sets which were the most prized and expensive, and nearly all this work was done by women. A few were elderly matriarchs of the trade. But most were young, their dexterous rosy fingers wielding their brushes with startling speed and total accuracy. As always with work done mainly by women, I learned, it was ill-paid. But then it was part of a low-cost, low-wage industry.

There were many famous names in pottery making –
Davenport and Minton, Spode and Elers, Doulton and
Copeland, Whieldon and Astbury – but few if any owners
became millionaires or even really rich men. Josiah Wedgwood
was the outstanding success story because it was he who
turned a farm industry of craftsmen into a national, indeed
international, business of large-scale production for a mass
market. He was the first to have a display room in London,
to catch the 'carriage trade' and his new Etruria Works, built
in the 1770s, was the first modern pot-bank. He built himself
a fine classical house alongside it – the Wedgwoods were
enthusiastic pioneers of the classical revival. Etruria itself was
the symbol of their devotion to the shapes and patterns,
colours and textures of ancient Rome. Those who lived there
called themselves Etruscans. An old photograph taken in the
1880s shows the Wedgwood mansion against a background of
bottle-shaped ovens belching smoke, with another group of
industrial buildings in the foreground. There was a park and
garden. But the smoke proved too much for the younger
generation of Wedgwoods and they removed to the countryside. So Etruria no longer had a family house in my day and
the only sign of gracious living was a group of trees called
Etruria Grove, where you could pick blackberries and, if you
looked hard, wild raspberries in season.

Keeping down costs was paramount in the trade. Mr
Thrower explained to me how the bottle ovens evolved. 'Ta
save muny, dost see – all simple like, just big space to stack
pots, furnace and funnel wiv draft to gerrout smoak. The
owner decided 'ow it would be, and t'shape depended on
t'pots he was firing. We used ter buildem oursells till recently.
No architect-like, nothen like that. A good bank'll last thirty
years, then we pullen down and put up anither. Aye. Ah 'elped
ter build many a bank.' In effect, the potteries, under the

Longton pot-banks

direction of a master potter, built their own works. But Mr Thrower was gloomy about the future. He said, 'Coal-firing is finished, they say. A while back [it was in 1927] they started firing by electrics and put oop two furnaces in Shelton. Aye. Then, a few years ago, they started to fire kilns with gas. There must be a dozen now. They will 'ave it it's saving but ah doan't know. There's still nine hundred of the old bottles but ah dassent swear 'ul build more.'

What fascinated me, and pleased my father, was that no two ovens were exactly alike, even if built at the same time for the same purpose. The curve of the shoulder, the width of the bases, the height of the chimney top – all were variable and each combination was unique. The odd straight chimney provided a contrast. It was a romantic skyline which gave me endless delight, to contemplate and to draw; and a skyline, for all its devotion to Mammon, punctuated by church towers and spires. And, in its own way, pot making was art.

My father said on this occasion, and I heard him say it again with variations, that he had faith in art, especially art of everyday things. 'The problem, Little Paul, is to debestialise man, to turn him from a destructive creature into a civilised and creative one. For four years in France I witnessed the three most intelligent peoples in Europe, the British, the French and the Germans, devote themselves to destroying each other by every means their ingenuity could devise. Do you follow me?'

'Oh yes,' I said, 'tell me about the war' [he had never mentioned it before in my hearing].

'No, I will not tell you about the war. I had enough living through it without talking about it now. But I'll tell you this, Little Paul. The destructiveness in human beings can be mitigated – that means made less – if the everyday things in their lives are made beautiful. Beauty is the enemy of violence and war and crime. It is an aspect of God, as St Thomas

Aquinas says. If people live in well-designed houses, have simple furniture which strives for elegance, and eat off plates and drink from cups which have fine shapes and beautiful patterns and colours, their characters will be softened and refined, and their behaviour will improve. So it's up to us to provide these things and that's what the Potteries ought to do in its particular sphere.'

I have summarised my father's argument. He spoke as an enthusiast, his words were complex and eloquent, and much was above my head. He, like my mother, never 'talked down' to his children. He expected me to follow, however stumblingly, and indeed I did. In later years I recognised his viewpoint as springing from the Arts and Crafts movement, going strong when he was a child, and ultimately from the views of Ruskin and William Morris. I am more sceptical than he was, now, but he believed his words, passionately and sincerely. The thesis gave him a vocation and an aim in life, and he passed it on to his pupils.

Before showing me his school, we passed the Wedgwood Institute, a noble building with much highly decorative terracotta on its façade, with figures from the pottery trade. 'See those low-reliefs,' he said. 'Those are by Lockwood Kipling, who lived and worked here for a time. He loved this part of the world. Have the girls taken you to Rudyard Lake yet?'

'Oh yes, Daddy.'

'Well, then, when old Kipling had a son, he called him Rudyard, after the lake, and Rudyard grew up to become one of the greatest poets and storytellers of modern times.' I knew about Kipling: the *Just So* stories and the *Jungle Book*, parts of which my sisters had read to me. Later I was to read for myself *Plain Tales from the Hills*, still one of my favourite books.

I knew some of his poems, too, especially 'If', which my

mother used to recite. She told me, 'He had poor sight and wore thick glasses. So the other boys called him "gigs" or "gigger" after the gig lamps which horse carriages had when I was a girl.' I used to see Kipling as a man with huge lamps where his eyes ought to have been, shining hot lights on people. I was glad I didn't have to wear glasses.

The Art School, nearby in Queen Street, was big, noisy and echoing. My father loved it. He saw it as a great engine of civilisation. When he got there and hung his hat in his office, he always donned an overall, 'to get down to work': sometimes white, sometimes brown, depending on which part of the school he intended to spend his time in. He despised 'admin' and tried to get through it quickly. He wanted to be out in the classroom, enthusing, exhorting, goading, praising and correcting. He loved his staff and they certainly loved him, but he must have been a trial to them at times, for he always wanted to take over the class and see what the boys and girls were up to. He was invariably elaborately polite, never lost his temper and tried hard not even to be cross. He did not call them 'children' or 'pupils', but always 'students', though they ranged from twelve to sixteen – very few came from families able to let them go on into the Senior Art School. These students were his 'treasures', lively potential geniuses who might go on to great things. It was his solemn responsibility to spot their particular talents, nurture and guide them. He said, 'There is in each human being an individual spark, put there by Almighty God, and if only we can find it and keep it alight, that human being will fulfil himself.' I also heard him say, 'Each of my students has the holy fire of art, in some medium and to some degree. I must bring it to a white heat by the wind of my enthusiasm; then it will become self-generating and produce – who knows? – marvels.'

There was a studio for drawing and another for poster art.

A workshop contained broad tables and facilities for etching, dry-point, lithography and steel engraving. Drawing on wood and woodcutting were then still important branches of art. All these things were taught. My father had to be most concerned with decorative and design skills, as these were the highroads to jobs in the pottery industry, and in printing and similar trades. And jobs were what everyone thought about, all the time. There were millions of unemployed men. I used to see them, hanging about in the streets, sometimes kicking a ball listlessly; more often doing nothing. Many had empty pipes, gripped in their jaws upside-down as a symbol of their plight. No money for tobacco, let alone beer. My father's overwhelming concern was that every one of his boys and girls, when they left at sixteen or often before, had a job to go to. He spent a lot of his precious time making friends with the managers of the works, and was in and out of Doulton's and Wedgwood, Minton's and Spode, Copeland's and Davenport's constantly, picking up the gossip, learning about 'new lines', which might provide 'openings', and singing the praises of his 'stars'.

He was a familiar figure in the district, bustling, always in a hurry, but trying never to seem so, visiting even the smallest potteries occasionally, 'just in case', and appreciative of their wares. He had a kindly word for the workmen as well as the manager, partly because he liked their ways and weird expressions, partly because 'you never knew': they might some day give him a key piece of information, which would mean a sure job for one of his students. 'Cast your bread upon the waters' was a favourite maxim of his; a puzzling one for me because I knew from experience that if you cast your bread on the waters of the Upper Park lake it was immediately gobbled by the swans or sank without trace. It was his pride, though he never boasted of it — that would not do — that he had always managed to get his alumni jobs in the 'trade', or at printers like Warwick Armstrong, and there are men and women still alive who will testify to his skill at placing them in 'safe jobs', thus assuring them, and often younger brothers and sisters, sustenance and hope in those hard times.

There was a locked room in the school, to which only he had the key, where supplies were kept: boxes of superb camel-hair brushes, pencils from Venus, Caran d'Ache and Castell, paints from Windsor & Newton, Reeves and Rowney's, pens from Waterman, long racks of marvellous drawing paper in various thicknesses, turps and linseed oil, inks and dyes, brilliant metallic drawing instruments, easels and stools of all kinds. He received innumerable samples of new lines from the major art manufacturers. These he regarded as legitimate perks for himself, artist friends and promising pupils, and in

Entrance to the Burslem School of Art

time I shared in this bounty. When he shut and locked the door he asked, 'Is there anything else you'd like to see?'

'Yes,' I said, 'the clay pit.'

'What? Why do you want to see that?'

'Mummy said that at all costs I was not to fall into it. I want to see it so I'll know what I'm not to fall into.'

'Sound sense,' said my father, laughing. 'So I'll show it to you.' It was not, disappointingly, a pit, but more like a huge vat or a wagon, made of zinc or perhaps lead, with tiny wheels so it could be trundled. It was full of china clay, kept continually malleable and moist by some kind of invisible watering system. I could not peer over the brim and had to stand on a stool to see within: a mass of grey-brown substance, glistening and sticky, begging to be moulded and shaped, and smelling delicious. Here was the raw material, the vital earth force on which the entire Potteries was built and from which everything emerged: fire and smoke, trade, profit and art.

My father's students all had to learn to model from clay. It was the key to the best jobs. It was also enormous fun and a wonderful training if you aspired to create art in three dimensions. The teenagers at the school loved it. It was, for them, much more free and easy than drawing, where my father imposed the strictest rules. No compasses. He could draw a perfect circle himself and taught them how to do it. The minimum rubbing out: 'Think first, hard,' he would say, 'then you won't need rubbers.' No rulers. With practice, he argued, the artist could learn how to draw straight lines with speed and proficiency. His rules of perspective were particularly stringent, and he also laid down maxims on shading, shadows, gloss, glitter, metallic sheen, drawing glass and glassware, and many other matters. Modelling of figures, let alone pots, had its rules too, and many of them. But it allowed, too, exuberance and creativity. Successful figures were baked and glazed, and my father would sometimes bring them home for our admiration. I still possess a little figure of myself, done from life by a student, showing me as a schoolboy: cap and jacket, satchel and trousers, a cheeky grin and legs spread wide to give the figure stability (always a prime concern when sculpting).

Many pottery firms produced figure work; indeed, a special kind of coloured figure was known as Staffordshire ware and is still eagerly collected in its eighteenth- and nineteenth-century versions. But Doulton's were the specialists. They not only employed fine designers and continually changed their archetypes; they also experimented with magnificent colours and deep, intense glazes, like their Chinese precursors. Doulton figures were, perhaps, the earliest form of art I learned to appreciate and, indeed, to handle. There were many examples in our house, gifts from the firm, I imagine, and my mother let me touch or even play with them when I was tiny – it was a rule in our household that art was for everyday use and never sacrosanct. My first art memory is of an enchanting mouse, coloured deep vermilion and purple – a masterpiece of glazing – sitting on a cube. I used to sing to this object 'Three Blind Mice', the first ditty I learned by heart. Then there was the 'Bengal Tiger', a lithe, splendid monster in orange and white, with wide-open jaws showing formidable teeth, and thrashing tail. My mother let me play with this beast while she recited 'Tyger, tyger burning bright / In the forests of the night', another poem I learned young from constant repetition.

Many porcelain figures (not all Doulton, of course; my father liked Chelsea, too, Nymphenburg and many others) passed through our house. I remember 'Elizabeth Fry', 'the genius of mercy' as my mother called her, designed by the sculptor Charles Vyse in 1913, and a beautiful 'Colombine', designed by Leslie Harradine, whom my father regarded as the most versatile of Doulton sculptors. This exquisite piece is still in my possession. Harradine created spirit flasks in the likeness of pre-1914 politicians, like Lloyd George, Balfour, Haldane and President Theodore Roosevelt — what would I give for such a set now! The Harradine figure which fascinated me, however, was 'The Bather', always displayed at home, high up on the shelves, with her brilliant blue-and-purple wrap showing. But if you turned her round she was naked and was known to the family as 'The Rude Lady'. Doulton's produced various 'daring' pieces over the years — 'Negligee', 'Circe', 'Carnival' and 'Siesta', for example — but Harradine's more popular lines played on sentiment rather than eroticism.

My mother's favourite, perhaps because of the name, was 'Sweet Anne', and she told me many stories about this early Victorian lady, who might have stepped out of *Cranford*. The most popular pieces of all were the various jesters designed by Charles Noke, for many years art director at Doulton's and (together with his son Jack Noke) well known to my father. He thought jesters rather feeble but loved Charles Noke's magnificent crimson 'Irving as Wolsey', which shone like a ruby in our drawing room. He also admired Noke's 'Spooks' as 'powerful'; it certainly frightened me.

It was a source of pride to my father that one of the Burslem students, Margaret Davies, universally known as Peggy, became a Doulton designer while still in her teens, and later produced some of the most magnificent pieces, including 'Eleanor of Provence', the 'Empress Matilda', 'Philippa of Hainault' and 'Margaret of Anjou', the 'She-wolf of France', as Shakespeare called her. The faces are superb and the high-gloss colours have never been equalled for depth and radiance. My father also thought highly of Eric Griffiths, who did some of the animal figures in our house and after the war created perhaps the most remarkable series of figures ever issued by an English potter. This was the thirteen American revolutionary soldiers wearing the uniforms of each of the thirteen states. The research was conducted in conjunction with the American Williamsburg Institute and only 350 sets were issued. The quality of the sculpture is exceptional and justifies my father's claim that 'Doulton's at its best – an important qualification – is a great artistic force'. Of course, he knew it in its glory days, the age of art deco, when great masters like Chiparus were around to influence the design and finish.

Some of my father's star students went on to become independent artists; others to design calendars, posters – a celebrated branch of art in the Thirties – and Christmas cards. This last was of particular importance to my father because, each November, he designed a family Christmas card himself and sent it out to all whom he and my mother loved best. In those days most artists put their hand to this kind of work, designing dinner and club menus, invitation cards for special galas, wedding cards, bookplates and countless other ephemera for which their skills came in handy. His cards were done in ink and wash, and lithographed. My father then painted each by hand, using watercolours – occasionally body colour too – and gold and silver paint. We all helped; or rather Clare and Elfride helped from the start, and I was allowed to join the team when I was about seven, in 1936. So it was like a medieval artistic family atelier, my father providing enthusiastic (sometimes a little tetchy) leadership, his children toiling at the less important bits. My mother accused him of 'turning the house upside-down' every year, but she was proud of the results. Sometimes as many as a hundred cards were sent out, and were much prized and kept. Perhaps there are still some in existence, over sixty years old now. Alas, I do not own one myself, and the pictures of cribs and Magi, shepherds and journeys into Egypt – and the marvellous lettering which adorned them – are all fading memories.

I regret, too, that I remember so little of the Potteries artistic community of which my father was a leading member. He was so devoted to his work, and to the anxious business of securing jobs for his students, that his own artistic interests were neglected. His beautiful and highly accurate line-and-wash drawings of churches, cathedrals and urban scenes always sold, when he had enough time to draw them. But when he was asked to do the drawings for a book about the Cotswolds he was obliged to decline: his work at the school did not leave him time to do the on-the-spot work required. So he passed the commission on to his friend Lowry. I still have the volume in which the curious line-and-wash drawings appeared.

To my father it was the height of felicity to get a fortnight off to spend sketching in the Low Countries, or a few weeks in Spain; there to draw churches to his heart's content. Every minute counted; he worked hard; and all was done 'expeditiously'. He did not look like an artist as a rule. He wore three-piece suits and sombre ties, as befitted a head-master in those days. The standard outfit for artists in the Thirties was a well-cut tweed jacket, no tie as a rule but a stock, a fawn waistcoat, often with brass buttons, and corduroy or cavalry twill trousers, worn tight on the legs. This rig was completed by a slouch or trilby hat, often with a broad brim, cocked over the left eye. The effect was smartish, upper-middle-class rustic. The prototypes of this sartorial fashion were 'Lamorna' Birch of the Newlyn-St Ives school and 'Alf' Munnings, the horse painter. One or two of my father's friends or colleagues dressed like this but the nearest he ever came to bohemianism, on his painting holidays, was a suede jacket topped by a beret – then much worn in Spain and France. Occasionally he wore a tweed suit, with waistcoat and plus-fours (golf) or plus-twos (walking). But he was happiest when working in an overall, which all the less flamboyant painters put on for studio garb.

My mother used to organise parties at the Art School, or jollifications as my father called them, sometimes in fancy dress, which artists in those days liked donning. She prepared the food or presided over the cooks, and saw to the music. My father always had a cinema show at these parties, in the lithography room, at which he ran through Disney films as he said the students could 'learn a few tricks from the artwork'. He confided to me once, 'Art is direct observation supplemented by tricks developed over the ages. But you must never use the word tricks.'

'Then why are you saying it, Daddy?'

'Because I like to tell you the truth.'

He had colleagues and friends round to our house to hold discussions in the Art Room. I was considered too young to attend these sessions and caught only glimpses of the personalities who attended. There was 'Tittensor', referred to as 'the Mighty Man', and 'a great power at Doulton's'. I expected to see a giant, possibly with a club and a fierce dog with a spiked collar round his neck. In fact, he was a smallish man in a raincoat with what was called a brown Derby on his head. Known as Harry, he designed a superb piece called 'The Parson's Daughter' with a demure face and wearing a patchwork skirt of brilliant colours, one of my mother's favourites. She referred to him as 'a real gentleman and you can't say that of many artists'.

Then there was 'Roscoe', who my father said was 'a coming man', but 'nervous' and 'doesn't push himself forward enough'.

I studied Roscoe intently to see the pushing forward forces at work and discern why he could not go further; but all he did was to scowl at the painting *Fishing Boats at Etretat* which hung in the hall.

There were 'the Farington ladies', as my mother called them: the widow of an artist (descended from the famous Joseph Farington, *'éminence grise* of the Royal Academy' in the early nineteenth century) and her 'talented daughter', Elvira. Another lady, Louise Brough, was also 'talented' and did a fine graphite drawing of my father, which I still possess. I suppose she was a 'coming woman', but I don't know whether she ever came. There was Susie Cooper, whom my father greatly admired, a designer of pottery in novel patterns and colours. She gave me a small brown bear she had modelled; lost, alas, during the war.

From snatches I heard, there was much talk of artists – 'Gunn', 'that fellow Nash', 'Bisley', 'Old Sickert' and 'Fancy Pants' – though who he was I never discovered. My father was obviously fond of someone he called 'the Circus Girl' or 'Laura', and talked about her until called to order by my mother who said, 'That's quite enough about Laura Knight.' My sisters, perhaps primed by my mother, were to my surprise highly critical of my father's artistic friends and used to give imitations of them, especially of the Farington ladies. Clare said many artists were 'circus freaks'. I saw no grounds for this comparison, except possibly in the case of 'Laura', whom I imagined standing on one leg on a high-stepping white pony. But Laura never appeared.

My father's efforts to turn out students equipped to fight their way in the world, and his energetic attempts to find them jobs, left him less and less time for his true career as an artist. I was aware of this and felt for him. I would have given any-thing in my power to lighten his burden and shared my

mother's concern about his health. But there was nothing I
could do, except listen to what he said and abide by his
instructions. He did some magnificent drawings nonetheless.
I have in my library today two of them: a pen and wash of
Bruges Cathedral, done with great panache but also with
meticulous accuracy, and a panoramic drawing of Canterbury,
done from a high position, in graphite, showing the cathedral
dominating the town, as it did in those days, dated August
1938. All is now transformed in that once delightful place and
my father's drawing, like so many he did then, is a historical
record of a view which has changed almost beyond recognition.

Most of his works were sold immediately, for he charged
modest prices, saying, 'No point in having the Art Room
cluttered.' So I possess few. He said, 'When I sell a drawing, I
think of you, Little Paul.' I was puzzled by this. But the next
time we went out together, to draw the high-spired church at
Hartshill, he said, 'I have plans to send you to boarding
school, Paul, to give you a good start in life. But that costs
money and I can't do it yet. Anyway, your mother won't hear
of it. She says her child should not be sent away to boarding
school until he is twelve. And you are eight, so you'll go this
autumn to St Joseph's, to the tender mercies of the Christian
Brothers. I don't suppose they are as bad as they're painted.
Indeed, they are excellent schoolmasters. I know the headmaster there, Brother Wall, and he is a sensible man.' So my
fate was sealed. In the meantime I drew furiously: soldiers,
tanks, battleships.

CHAPTER SEVEN
Treats and Tricks

I WAS DIVIDED in my mind about my mother's veto on my being sent away to school. On the one hand I wanted the excitement and drama of a boarding school: the only 'real' school according to the stories I had read, where the competition and friendships and rivalries of school life were at their most intense. On the other, her insistence that twelve was the earliest at which I could go was reassuring. I remembered Miss King's advice: 'Learn to box.' I had not yet learned. Besides, my friendship with my mother waxed even closer and more confiding as I grew older and she could open her mind to me more completely. I realised that I was becoming more important to her too, in the sense that I was her companion and trusty follower.

I loved going shopping with her. She had the gift of transforming the most routine trip into an adventurous expedition. Among her many aids to memory was a rhyme listing all the articles a housewife needed, beginning 'Tea, coffee, cocoa, lemons, butter, bacon, eggs' and going through all the items in the store cupboard. She used to sing it before leaving the house and at intervals between the shops to make sure nothing had been forgotten: 'More reliable than a written list.' She told me all about the Maypole, the Home & Colonial and the Co-Op, and which was best for what. They were the equivalent of today's Tesco and Waitrose. With no supermarkets, shopping could take time. At the Home & Colonial my mother would sit on a high stool at the counter, while the assistant (always male) in a spotless white apron going down to his feet and a white cap, got her purchases. Each was carefully spooned out with a silver shovel from huge bins in heraldic jars, weighed on a vast brass scale, then packaged into neat white or brown paper parcels, tied with string and made up with astonishing dexterity. I watched this process with insatiable fascination. I was particularly intrigued by the powerful bacon slicer, carefully adjusted to the precise thickness my mother desired, then set in monumental motion with a distinct hissing noise, as the rashers slid out.

Then came the climax, when the shop man added up the total, my mother paid, and bill and money were loaded into a mechanical device which was shot by wires into the cashier's pulpit high in the shop, to the ringing of a bell. The cashier (always a woman) returned the change in the same device, which shot down on to the counter, ting-a-ling. This ingenious ritual gave a wonderful sense of ceremony to the transaction and was pure joy to a child. Most shops delivered the goods in a special kind of pushbike with a small front wheel surmounted by an enormous basket, all propelled by strong teenage boys who whistled tunes from *The Merry Widow* and *Showboat*. ('Never whistle like an errand boy,' my mother warned, 'the habits of errand boys are to be avoided.')

My mother often took me by bus to Burslem when she went there on business to do with the Art School and its activities. She felt sorry for some of the younger, poorer students who 'looked as though they never got a proper breakfast' and would 'be lucky if they got a knife-and-fork tea when they reached home'. She gave them delicious sultana scones (pronounced 'skons') which she baked herself, and goosenagh cakes, a Lancashire speciality, sent to her in huge batches by her mother, known to us as Nana. Nana made about twenty different kinds of cakes, pies and biscuits, and had a grand baking day once a week for pure pleasure, for her children had long since grown up; and she sent the output in all directions, made up in skilful parcels by her husband (Papa to us), who had once run a delivery business, and was an expert in string, knots, wax seals and home-made glue.

But my mother said, 'I have no ambition to run a bakery.' All she made were scones, pies (apple, rhubarb, blackberry and damson, chiefly; occasionally pear and plum, and bilberries – best of all – when Clare found and picked them). She always baked a huge cake at Christmas and a dozen plum puddings, one for us, the others to be given away to poor families in the neighbourhood. Her thoughts constantly dwelt on the poor and how to help them out of her own exiguous housekeeping money. She always made, for instance, two cottage or shepherd's pies, one for us, one for 'the needy'. Delivering a gift of food was a delicate business, for Potteries people, even if in dire want, were fiendishly proud and had to be approached with tact.

My mother often used as an intermediary, as well as a source of information, Mrs Williams, who knew everything and seemed to be on friendly terms with everyone. She secretly told me stories of need, sickness, accidents and fights, of vendettas and rivalries, which my mother usually refused to listen to but which to me were a constant delight and source of horror. Some of these, of course, came from 'the Master', who had personal knowledge of dastardly doings in 'the Sheds', where the engines were kept, and heard of still worse affrays at 't'deep levels' of the pits. My mother said, 'You mustn't always take at face value what Mrs Williams tells you.'

Burslem landscape

'Why?'

'Oh, she's inclined to gild the lily, or rather deepen the chiaroscuro.' The remark was characteristically mysterious (to me), but I got the drift of it from my mother's equally characteristic facial expressions.

Money was certainly not plentiful in our house. My parents' priorities were church, education, charity and books. Food came low down the list, though we were never hungry. We had plenty of milk, eggs and butter from the Machins' farm. Fresh cream was a rarity. We always had roast beef on Sunday. Vegetables were delivered by, according to my mother, 'a rather ruffianly man' called Potts (a common name in the district, as was Potter, Potterton and Pottsby). She had once caught him using our downstairs loo, next to the coal cellar,

without permission. I rather liked him because he had a friendly horse called Sally and gave me a red apple from time to time. Only at Christmas did we have grapes and Chinese oranges, wrapped in silver paper. There were Seville oranges for making marmalade, however, and sweet Valencia ones with thin skins, and sweet, thick-skinned Jaffas 'from the Holy Land'. 'These were the oranges Jesus ate,' I was told.

I don't ever remember having fresh peaches. They came in tins, as did fruit salad, cream (both thick, and thin Carnation Milk), mandarin oranges, pineapple lumps and apricots. Plums were plentiful and so were damsons, made into jam (I did the stirring). Figs we never had, except in tiny quantities, dried, at Christmas. Strawberries and raspberries were treats in early summer. Apples we never lacked. Avocados had not yet been 'discovered'. Corn cobs were unknown in England then. So were Chinese and Indian food, at least in Staffordshire. Italian food was never eaten, though some children said they had had tinned spaghetti. But this was regarded as 'disgusting'. We had plenty of lettuce, tomatoes and cucumber – too much, in fact.

We liked soup but the range we got was limited and it was a source of discontent for me that we never got the crackers in it which Shirley Temple sang about in her movie *Animal Crackers*. She was, however, held up to me as a model of good manners: 'Shirley Temple never complains about her food and always smiles at table.' Another model was my near-contemporary Princess Margaret Rose, as she was then called: 'Princess Margaret Rose is never late for meals', 'Princess Margaret Rose has clean hands at all times'. When, many years later, I said to her, 'You were represented to me as a paragon,' she replied, 'Well, I *was* well-behaved then.'

We had no frozen food but a lot was tinned: pears, beans, corned beef, ham, meat loaf (unpopular), Spam (very popular), salmon. In the whole of my childhood I never tasted fresh salmon, lobster, oysters, crab or mussels. The last were listed by my mother as 'unhealthy', along with veal, mutton pies, tripe (joyfully consumed by potters), liver and kidneys. We had kippers but smoked salmon was unheard of. There were always plenty of things to spread on slices of bread ('the staff of life' my mother called it) or toast, made at the fire with toasting forks, for no one had electric toasters then. These included various kinds of potted meat, fish and anchovy paste, and Marmite (dismissed by my father as 'vegetarian rubbish'; he preferred Bovril or, better still, a brand he had discovered on a voyage to Australia called Vitamite. As this was unobtainable in England, he declined the condiment altogether, as was no doubt his intention all along). The range of jams and marmalades was infinite, mostly home-made, my mother's pots being massively supplemented by jars from Nana who, my mother said, 'would turn anything into jam, not excluding turnips and old pyjamas'. I took this literally and the next time I saw Nana asked, 'Have you made any pyjama jam?'

She looked bewildered, then said, 'Has Annie been making fun of me again?' I was beginning to realise that my mother made (gentle) fun of everyone, sooner or later. It was like being a child (I came to see) of Jane Austen.

The range of drinks, taken last thing at night, included not only Horlicks, to ward off midnight starvation, but Ovaltine, Benger's Food (unpopular), Bourneville chocolate, cocoa, malted milk and egg-nog. If we were constipated we were made to drink a concoction called Senna Tea, brewed from pods. I was sometimes obliged to down a tablespoonful of a nauseous syrup called Cod-liver Oil and Malt, and when we had colds my mother made an excellent hot lemonade, well spiced. We never had coffee, though a popular drink for children's elevenses was a feeble imitation, imported from colonial India, called Camp Coffee, a dark-brown liquid which came in a bottle showing a sahib and his tent on the label. My mother sometimes mixed it for me with cocoa, calling the result 'cofco'.

I was vaguely aware that Authority regarded the popular English diet as unhealthy. It was indeed shaped by political forces: the desire to keep food as cheap as possible and to import the maximum amount from the Empire. Studying, as I did, the newspaper cartoons with passionate interest, I noticed that an entity called 'Home Farming' lived in a place labelled 'the Doldrums'. The cartoons by Strube in the *Daily Express* (owned by what my father called 'that Imp of Satan, Beaverbrook'; I longed to see him) featured a tall, weary man in corduroy trousers labelled 'Idle Acres'. Campaigns were set on foot to consume 'home products'. Arthur Machin used to talk about them when he drove me in his trap. One day he told me, 'Hast 'eard? They've gorra Milk Bar in Buzlum?' I told my mother and the next time we went to Burslem she took me there.

It was on the Market Place, a brand-new art deco set-up with plenty of chromium, glass and bright colours – apple-green, cherry-red and ivory-white – with waitresses in high caps behind the bar, at which you sat on important stools. It was in every way the latest thing, said to be by the same designer who decorated the *Queen Mary*, the great nautical wonder of those times. But for me the real miracle was its speciality, Vanilla Milk Shake. Milk shakes had existed in America since before the Great War: my father said he had sampled them in 'New York Drug Stores' as far back as 1910. But they were quite unknown in Staffordshire until this amazing Milk Bar, in itself an unheard-of innovation, served them. It came from out of a glittering machine, all frothy and frosted, and from the first sip I realised I was tasting what my mother jokingly called 'the Milk of Paradise' ('Kubla Khan' was one of her favourites). It was subtle, refined, ultra-sophisticated and altogether delicious. I had never tasted anything so good in my life. I made it last as long as I possibly could, until even my mother grew impatient. As it cost sixpence, it was as far beyond my means as vintage Krug and I assumed I would never have another. So I sipped and sipped, like an old don savouring ancient port. Outside, I recall, a Salvation Army band played. As part of their campaign against demon drink, they saw the Milk Bar as an ally.

I sampled another magic taste not long afterwards. Although my mother dutifully went to Burslem when required, she really hated the place. Hanley was her preferred choice for an expedition. Though a Potteries town like the rest, it had expanded rapidly in the nineteenth century and had become the shopping centre of the entire district; the only place, in my mother's view, which could remotely compare with Manchester. There were half a dozen shops she pronounced 'enterprising', and it had an air of bustle and pleasure singularly lacking in the other Potteries towns. Let us not exaggerate. It was just as dirty as the rest. From the centre, insofar as it had one, it was only a step to the old bottle kilns and chimneys. But in one of its spacious emporia it was possible to forget, for a few minutes, that pots were the be-all and end-all of life. There was an art gallery, a theatre, a modern cinema, a Grand Hotel and the office of the *Staffordshire Sentinel.*

My mother liked to visit four or five shops, then settle down into a comfortable chair in the tea-room at Huntbach's, her favourite. There was a little string orchestra, and neat pretty waitresses in brown-and-white uniforms handed round cakes from many-tiered stands. The first time I went with her she encouraged me to have a macaroon, and from the initial mouthful I realised that I had discovered a gastronomic delight on a level with vanilla milk shake, something which melted in my mouth with a taste of indefinable sweetness and glory. For the first time in my life, I think, I used a figure of speech: 'It's as though it was made by an angel,' I said.

My mother laughed. 'All it needs is ground almonds, white of egg and sugar. Your friend Lukie could make it, except he'd add a fourth ingredient, dirt.'

On these occasions she treated herself to a poached egg on toast and gave the waitress elaborate instructions on how it was to be made. My mother always set a high standard of abstemiousness. I never saw her eat a cake ('too rich') or a pudding ('indigestible') or much meat-and-potato stuff ('too greasy'). She ate like a bird, as she would say, and lived into her nineties, working all her life and expending a degree of energy in relation to nutriment that defied all the laws of nature. But one lightly poached egg on a golden slice of toast was a thing she relished. Like Mr Woodhouse, she thought it 'not unwholesome'. I loved to see her happy and seated comfortably at Huntbach's, waited on (for a change), in a faint aroma of Earl Grey. With me in attendance to listen to her quiet but entertaining comments on the other tea imbibers, she was a contented soul.

My mother and I went to Hanley to shop and did not hang around its outskirts, which were insalubrious. She told me that the district had been ruined by the needs of the 'Granville earls' for cash. The first Earl owned virtually all the land, though he never lived on his estates. He was a gambler and in the 1820s had once lost £23,000 at Crockford's in a single night of madness. The French card-sharpers in Paris knew him as 'le Wellington des Joueurs' (this took some explaining to me). So he and his son, the second Earl Granville, had exploited the mineral wealth of Hanley for all it was worth, to 'raise the ready' as they called it. They sank the dreaded Deep Pit and many others. They opened a racecourse but it didn't pay; so they sank the Racecourse Pit on its site. They dug clay and built the Shelby Pottery. They started five flint mills and set up a tile works. They hugely expanded the iron-workings at Shelton and the second Earl eventually formed the Shelton Iron, Steel and Coal Company. My mother said he 'never set foot in the hell he created, but if you ask whether he went to the real one in the end, your opinion is as good as mine. He was a chuckle-headed fellow with curly hair like yours.'

She said parts of Hanley were 'riddled with subsidence' from shallow coal-workings. Potteries at Etruria had sunk nine feet below the level of the nearby canal (you could see that plainly). She showed me slanting houses and the street where a man, 'before the war', had simply disappeared into a black hole that had suddenly opened and never been seen again. 'They had to hold his funeral without him.' Granville was 'a figure of ill omen'. She said he 'got a telegram announcing that his favourite niece had been struck dead by lightning and read it out in the middle of a Cabinet meeting. Mr Gladstone said an impromptu prayer.' Also, 'He was riding with Bishop Wilberforce when the bishop was thrown from his horse and died instantly.' I don't know where my mother got this curious information, some of which was undoubtedly true.

My father said, 'Without Granville, Hanley would have been a dead duck,' an expression which left me baffled.

Whether the Granvilles had anything to do with the great

The giant gasworks outside Hanley

gasworks which was built outside Hanley I was not told. It was boasted of as 'a masterpiece of gas engineering' and one of the largest in the country. My sisters and I saw it twice a day when the train passed it just outside Etruria Station and it never failed to fill me with deep thoughts about industry. The main tower was 'rigid', but two towers nearby moved up and down inside their frames in accordance with how much gas they contained. They were at different levels each day and I was anxious to spot one or other actually moving, but never did. A man on the train, observing my interest, said, 'If that lot went oop, then bang goes t'entire Potteries. I reckon ter German bombers 'ave already marked it as prime target, dost tha' know?'

This was the first news I had received about German bombers and I asked my father if it was true. He sighed deeply and said, 'God forbid!'

The summer before I went to St Joseph's High School my mother and sisters and I travelled to Lytham to stay with her parents, Nana and Papa. This was always a great treat for all of us. First came the train. We travelled on our Loop Line to Longport and changed there on to the express, which took us through Crewe, the famous and busy junction. My mother delighted to sing us a song about it:

> Oh, Mr Porter, what shall I do?
> I want to go to Birmingham
> But they're taking me on to Crewe.
> Send me back to London
> As quickly as you can.
> Oh, Mr Porter, what a silly girl I am!

Crewe was in Cheshire and we passed through fields with

immense herds of cows. I loved a big sign, carried by two life-size wooden men, which read 'Drink More Milk'. Warrington, which my mother dismissed as 'a disreputable town, neither one thing nor the other' – what the 'things' were I don't know to this day – had a huge factory and coal mines, giant wheels spinning. It stood on the border of Cheshire and Lancashire, and once the train pulled out of the station my mother said, 'Back in civilisation again.' Wigan, the next stop, was an epitome of industrial Lancashire and from the train we could see below endless streets of back-to-back houses, two-up, two-down, in dark-red brick with slate roofs. They were beginning to modernise them, even in those days, and they have long since been pulled down – another vanished landscape. My mother, very perceptive about such things, grasped that people actually preferred unmodernised terrace houses to modern council flats because 'no sensible person lives in a flat if she can have a house to be proud of'. She added, 'The sign of proper pride is a well-scrubbed front step, a polished brass knocker and clean window-panes.'

At that time, though we did not know it, of course, the young George Orwell was living in the town, gathering material for his book *The Road to Wigan Pier*. The conditions he described were horrific and I certainly had no idea people lived such straitened and miserable lives. My mother knew a lot about poverty from her schoolteaching days but she took a more cheerful view of human life than Orwell did. 'So long as people have a faith and a family,' she told me, 'they can be happy, and if they get a bit of an education too, they can rise.' She pointed out people wearing clogs – almost unknown in the Potteries but common in Wigan. 'They're wooden and you get used to them but they give you corns.' She told me about the 'knocker-up man' who woke the miners and the mill girls in the morning by tapping the upper windows of the terrace

houses with a special long stick. She sang a song about Wigan
Pier:

> Hast heard of Wigan Pier?
> It's bracing, never fear.
> A long way from the sea,
> Maybe —
> But fine for thee and me!

There was some Manchester malice in this ditty, which had
several verses I have forgotten, dwelling on the pier's salubrious
site on the canal. My mother said that there was such a pier,
though 'really a canal jetty, for tying the barges to — and it fell
down long ago'.

    The next stop was Preston, where we changed into the little
Lytham train. My mother was fond of Preston, where began
the north part of Lancashire from which Nana came. She
pointed out to me the immense spire of the Catholic church,
right next to the railway line, built by Joseph Hansom, who
designed the convent at Stoke and Priory House. She had
another little song for Preston, which went,

> Poor Preston, proud people.
> Low church, high steeple.

    I noticed the different cries of the porters at these stations.
Before the arrival of loudspeakers, porters perfected stentorian
platform cries, with significant variations. Thus, 'This is
Crewe. Crewe Station. *Crewe.*' And, 'Here is Warring*ton*.
Warring*ton.*' 'Wigan. Wigan. *Wigan.*' 'Preston Station. Pres-ton-
Station.' I loved Lytham Station. It was famous for its display
of flowers and shrubs, its inlaid pattern of pebbles and its
ever-fresh whitewash. My grandparents lived nearby in

Westby Street and the porter trundled our luggage there in his trolley, a service for which he was rewarded by my mother's smile, for he never accepted a tip. The house was small but delightful. It had an unforgettable smell mingling baking cakes and bread, fresh paint, flowers and polish. Everything shone.

My grandfather was a handyman of infinite resource and many of the amenities in the house, and much of the furniture, were of his making. He had a workshop at the end of the garden where he kept his carpentry bench, lathes and vices, rows of gleaming chisels and tools, and many pots of strong-smelling glues, paints, oils and chemicals. While Nana cooked and baked, sewed and darned, ironed and prettified the house, tending her pots of plants and shrubs, Papa sawed and chiselled, chipped and painted. They had raised a large family and now they enjoyed a busy retirement. They seemed to me, even at the time, an exceptionally happy couple, each character fitting into the other, like one of Papa's carefully glued joints. He was calm, quiet, soft-spoken. I never heard his voice raised. He was modest and self-effacing, extremely courteous in manner, a little formal in the way old-fashioned Mancunians were. He always called me Master Paul. He said, 'You are an artist, like your father. I am a craftsman. I won't teach you carpentry because you don't need to make things. That's my job. Your job is to design. So design me a little bookshelf and I will make it.' This was an exhilarating idea and I set to at once, with some help from Elfride; and in due course the little bookshelf was made and I put into it my small collection: *Bevis, The Adventures of Tom Sawyer, Our Island Story, Treasure Island, Robinson Crusoe* and Lamb's *Tales from Shakespeare.*

In those days nearly all the pavements of Lytham were patterned with white, black and brown pebbles from the seashore. The shops were shielded from the sun by glass and

wood (sometimes iron) arcades, brightly painted in green and
white. All was clean, with a light dusting of sand from the sea:
no smuts. We wore sandals and white ankle socks, khaki
shorts and white shirts or blouses. I got a penny a day pocket
money: riches. The pride of Lytham was its green, which
seemed to stretch for miles, between the little town and the
sea. On the green was a large, white-washed windmill, a
wonder to me, though it was no longer used to grind corn.
There was a fine paddling pool, mussel beds, a good sandy
beach, sandhills and a small pier. On the green, in summer, a
wood and canvas theatre was set up, and pierrots and pierrettes
performed in the afternoon. They told jokes which even I
could understand. 'I say, I say, why did the chicken cross the
road?' 'Because the traffic lights say go?' 'No, no, no, try again.'
'Because the trains aren't running?' 'No, no, no. I say, what an
ass you are! No, *to get to the other side!*' 'Ha, ha!' 'Ha, ha!' we all
roared.

The great events of the season, for children, were the
competitions run by newspapers. The *News Chronicle* held a
'spot-the-man' chase involving a sinister figure called Lobby
Ludd, of whom a rather fuzzy photo, in a trilby pulled down
over his eyes, was published. Each day he was in a different
seaside resort. If you spotted him, you were to arm yourself
with a copy of the paper and say, 'You are Lobby Ludd and I
claim the *News Chronicle* award.' Any deviation from this
formula was fatal to your chances. When Lobby Ludd was in
Lytham we never saw him, but we mistakenly accused several
men of being him. One swore, one gave Clare a kiss and one
handed me a penny. The *Daily Mail* sand competition, held in
nearby St Anne's, was more to our taste. Younger ones like me
had to build sandcastles or similar buildings. We all got tin
boxes of toffees and the winner a train set or talking doll.

Clare and Elfride, of course, went in for the older competition, which was to make a beautiful pattern of shells and pebbles framing a message which had to contain the words 'Daily Mail'. Both my sisters won first prizes at different times – Clare by including superb displays of seaweed forming a cricket pitch with the slogan 'For Fair Play read the *Daily Mail*' and Elfride for her imitation of a *Mail* front page, with the title *Daily Mail* over the headline 'The Paper for Clever Boys and Girls'. This sycophancy in both cases netted £2, a vast sum in those days. Their pictures and winning exhibits appeared on the Saturday back page of the paper – a trophy long preserved and now, I fear, lost.

Staying in Lytham, on this occasion, exorcised a terror. When I was smaller, on a similar visit, my sisters had taken me on a walk through the Avenue, an arcade of trees which contained a pond. This stretch of water had a bright-green covering of algae called Ginny Green-teeth, which I was told would swallow me up and drown me if I fell in. Ginny Green-teeth terrified me and I did drawings of her in an unsuccessful attempt to banish my fears. But this year, on our annual walk to the danger spot, I suddenly realised that it was all nonsense. 'Why,' I said, 'it's just weeds.'

'That's what I told you,' said Clare, 'but you were too scared to listen.' I pondered on this deception, or self-deception, and realised that I had passed an important turning point in my life and could face the big school with fortitude.

Going there in September was helped by the fact that I still travelled with my sisters. I had further to walk up Hartshill and over the top down into Trent Vale. The school was near the summit, almost new, and had all the latest facilities: chemistry and physics laboratories, a beautiful music room, an art room with gigantic studio windows reaching up to and into the roof, and a huge gym, the envy of Miss King. I was equipped with a new and heavy leather school bag, new grey shorts, a black blazer with scarlet piping and a black-and-red cap. Brother Wall's greeting was brief, but portentous: 'Are you a serious boy?'

'Yes, Brother.'

'Good. Stay so and you will prosper here.'

The brothers wore long black robes, reaching to their ankles (but with ordinary black trousers underneath), tightly gathered at the waist by a broad black band and with a slit down the front of their blouse-like black top. Inside the slit reposed their strap, a heavy instrument of sewn leather, with a shaped handle, ready for use at all times and administered on the hand with vigour. In Ireland they were notorious for their constant use of corporal punishment – never on the behind, however, let alone the bare behind, regarded as the depth of immorality. Dublin wags said the Christian Brothers and the Sisters of Mercy (who looked after, and beat, the girls) were the most un-Christian and merciless creatures in creation. There is an accurate account of a Dublin school run by the brothers in James Joyce's *Portrait of the Artist as a Young Man*. No doubt in England the brothers had to be more circumspect in their behaviour. They still used the strap a great deal and not just on the hands. The only one of them who exhibited signs of sadism, however, was the old man who taught carpentry. He hit clumsy boys with pieces of wood and squeezed their arms in a painful manner. He was a repellent and fearsome man whom I regarded with horror. (I should add that in the whole of my schooldays, spent entirely under Catholic priests, brothers or nuns, this was the only occasion I came across or heard about suspicious behaviour to undo children.)

With all their faults the Christian Brothers were devoted and highly professional schoolmasters, whose one aim was to do their best for the boys committed to their care. In Ireland they took great pride in spotting talent from the poorest families and transforming a clever boy in ragged clothes (often with no shoes in those days) into university material, becoming in due course a doctor, lawyer or other professional man. They were probably the finest nurturers of talent in Europe, not excluding the Jesuits, for their single-minded pursuit of pushing the poorest to the top, or at least to middle-class respectability. Their object was in no way qualified, as it was with the Jesuits, by the parallel aim of cultivating society and running schools for the well-connected. The brothers were particularly assiduous at teaching science and mathematics, for a high proportion of their cleverest boys became doctors, engineers and research workers.

So I was soon plunged into the world of algebra and logarithms, test tubes and retorts, statics and dynamics. Latin was taken more lightly but the brothers insisted we learn to write clearly and elegantly, and in correct grammatical English. I slaved over copybooks and parsed sentences until everything from gerunds to ablative absolutes fell into place and became second nature. A sweet baby-faced brother called O'Meara coached me in difficult subjects with extraordinary patience, and a stern, tall fellow called O'Connor showed me the way in maths and science. Neither ever strapped me, though scarcely a day went by without me seeing their fearsome instruments used. Boys did not mind. It made life dramatic, and they preferred it to lines, detention, sarcasm and shouting.

Brother Wall, like my father, was hag-ridden by the fear of his boys not getting jobs when they left at sixteen or eighteen. He was particularly anxious that the school have a good name with employers. This meant that behaviour while wearing the highly distinctive school uniform had to be impeccable, or as nearly so as he could make it by threats and terror. Soon after I joined the school he announced, at morning assembly, 'Attention all boys! Two of you have behaved in a SCANDALOUS and DISREPUTABLE manner, while in school uniform. You have been observed FIGHTING and heard SWEARING in public on a vehicle owned by the City of Stoke-on-Trent Municipal Services! Come forward those two boys and declare your ignominy!' No one moved. 'Ah! Ye'll be cowardly will ye?' (Brother Wall's Irish accent tended to come to the fore when he was angry.) 'Well, I have news to communicate to you wicked boys. Your identities are KNOWN TO ME! Now will ye come forward, ye unmitigated RASCALS?' At length two tall hangdog louts moved to the front of the hall. 'Ah-ha, is it you, Cartlidge and Tinkersclough! Come on to the platform where we can all see you! Stand under the picture of Blessed Ignatius Rice, our founder, so he can see you suitably disciplined!' A stern whacking followed. One of the boys cried. I was alarmed and disgusted by the episode, and wondered how I would endure such an exposure.

I shared my anxieties with my mother, who repeated, 'Don't cross your bridges before you come to them. I don't suppose you will ever be strapped, as you're a clever imp at avoiding trouble.' She was right; but my worries continued. I always found school a worrying place; indeed, I find life a worrying state.

My mother, by contrast, had an optimistic nature, which she handed on to her daughter Clare. (Elfride was more like me.) She had no high opinion of the Irish and was certainly not scared by 'a pack of Christian Brothers who are lucky to have shoes on their feet', as she put it. She always helped me with my homework if she felt like it, though it was strictly forbidden, and kept me at home if she thought I looked 'peaky' or was in danger of 'overdoing things'. Then she would write a superb letter of excuse in her beautiful, clear, elegant handwriting, cunningly written with all her inside knowledge of how a schoolteacher's mind worked. She had Brother O'Meara and Brother O'Connor to tea, and charmed and flattered them. She was also nice to Sergeant Hammond, our sports instructor. She told him she wanted me to learn to box, but I was on no account to get hurt in the process. He scratched his head and said, 'Well, Madam, that's a bit of a contradiction, I fear.'

'Well, Sergeant, not hurt more than is absolutely necessary. I shall hold you responsible!'

'I will do my best, Ma'am,' said the Sergeant, a guardsman who was no doubt accustomed to dealing softly with the imperious wives of officers.

At my first boxing class I received a powerful blow in the solar plexus, which quite paralysed me with shock. But after that I fared better, acquired rudimentary skills, and was soon boxing with unusual ferocity and some success. The two most powerful boys in my class, 'Backer' Bailey, a large boy of notable strength, and 'Snake' Snape, a smallish boy of fiendish temper and courage, both learned to leave me alone.

My mother triumphed in a manner so outrageous on one occasion that I hesitate to recount it even now. The first showing of *Snow White and the Seven Dwarfs* in the grand cinema at Hanley was a local event of some importance. She was determined to go to it and take me too. Brother Wall was equally determined to prevent any boy from his school going on a weekday, taking time off and shaming the school by flagrant truancy. 'Pay attention, boys! On no account whatsoever are you to see this cinematic exhibition in school time! Ye hear? I'm told it's sorcery anyway. Whether or not that be so, no boy is to go on Wednesday, or he will be detected and punished as surely as night follows day, believe ye me!' In a few cases this dread edict was disobeyed. Mine was one. But my mother had delivered the next day (by hand of Clare) a letter to Brother Wall of such sweetness and ingenuity, explaining her concern about my 'fragile health' without at any point telling a deliberate falsehood – let alone admitting she had shamelessly taken me to a movie, well concealed in an enveloping garment, which made it difficult to tell whether I was boy, girl or old age pensioner – as to disarm all suspicion. The next morning I witnessed condign punishment meted out on the offenders, while I remained safe and innocent thanks to my mother's duplicity. She said, 'I don't see why you should not see that wonderful film. It is uplifting and artistic, and the songs are delightful. *Sorcery* indeed! Those brothers live too much out of the world for their own good.'

My father knew nothing of this scandalous defiance of pedagogic authority. My sisters, even Clare, were shocked: '*We* would *never* have been allowed to go. It's one law for girls and one for boys.'

To which my mother retorted, 'Dr Johnson rightly observed that the law gives little power to women since nature has given them so much.' This was not a maxim my mother would have quoted in any other context; indeed, behind her carefully maintained support of order and the status quo there was a proto-feminist concealed.

It was true, as she said, 'You poor children don't get many treats.' Like other people of her generation she believed the good, spacious days had ended with the Great War and that those brought up after it were somehow deprived. Her tales of the jollifications before August 1914 were endless. She and her particular friends, Gertie Curly and Aggie Andrews, seem to have gone to constant parties – 'and of course we had more brothers altogether to squire us!' But Clare and Elfride were anxious to get to university and make careers for themselves. I don't recall them ever talking about boys.

Tom did no squiring: he was lost in a world of science and mechanics, of motorbikes and electric circuits, transmitters and specialist magazines. It was the eve of the electronic age with radar, the first mainframe computers and jet flight just over the horizon: an exciting age for someone of his aptitude to live in. He had just left school, having failed to get a scholarship to university – for his interests did not coincide with the curriculum at any point – and was working at Boots the Chemist as a dispenser. He wanted, he told me, to 'get away into the world' and in the meantime longed for the world war which would make it possible and which many said they could see coming (Marshall's parents, for instance, both damned as 'reds' by my father!).

We made our own pleasures: drawing, writing, above all, reading. My sister Clare got on with her epic poem. Elfride started a story. I did cartoons. Our reading was wide: my mother complained that my father 'opened the floodgates to books, which are inundating the entire home'. No restrictions were placed on our reading.

But it was Tom who introduced me to Dickens. He had a habit of repeating phrases and sayings used by some of the characters in a most ingenious and startling way, which not only made me laugh but appealed strongly to my instincts as a caricaturist. He said to me, indeed, 'Dickens *was* a caricaturist but in words.' It began with the Fat Boy: 'I wants to make your flesh creep'; went on with Sergeant Bagnet: 'Discipline must be maintained!' and Miss Trotwood's 'Janet! *Donkeys!*' and reached a climax with Weller's 'It's over and can't be helped, as they always says in Turkey when they cuts the wrong man's head off', which reduced me to convulsions of mirth. I learned to run like Trotty Veck, to rub my hands like Uriah Heep and say 'I 'opes I'm 'umble' and to squeak 'Youse a brimstone chatterer' like Old Smallweed and throw a cushion at his wife. I chanted with Mrs Gamp, 'Rich folk may ride on camels but it ain't so easy for them to see out of a needle's eye,' though I had no idea what it meant, and I loved to say with the pawnbroker, 'Oh, my liver and lights! Oh, will you take this weskit?' though what he meant was a mystery. I also repeated, over and over again, weird phrases like 'There's milestones on the Dover Road', a dark saying of Mr F's Aunt in *Little Dorrit*, and Silas Wegg's revelation: 'I generally reads on gin-and-water' — until the last was forbidden by my mother. 'I don't know where you get hold of such shocking catchphrases,' she said.

'It's Dickens, Mummy.'

'So much the worse. Dickens deserted his wife.'

I was silent. I did not reveal I had also learned Mr Mantoline's lament: 'I am always turning the mangle in a damnation mill. My life is one damned horrid grind.' I was enjoying the freedom newly bestowed on me by the world of books.

CHAPTER EIGHT

The Road to Mow Cop

THE POTTERIES IN those days was a collection of overgrown villages bonded into an industrial smoke furnace by greed and the love of art. In a sense villages they remained for the countryside *was* still close, on all sides. Arnold Bennett, in his *Journals*, wrote that you could sense 'the smell and declivity of the hills beneath the stone pavements'. That was still true in my time, the Thirties. Even the polluted streams had an undertone of the babbling brook. I had only to walk to the end of Queen's Avenue to see green fields. But there was, as it were, a no-man's-land before you got to them. One of my earliest memories was a curious range of low hills, made of stones, at the bottom of Tunstall's built-up area. They had been dumped there by builders and road makers whose contract had not been extended, a common sight in the slump. I loved this field of stone heaps and visited it daily if I got the chance. It had a certain mystery, to me at least. But I vaguely felt it was incongruous, that it ought not to be there. Sometimes, out-of-work miners squatted there on their haunches, playing an illegal game, pitch and toss. They glanced up guiltily when they realised they were being watched, then swore at me: incomprehensible, deep-throated oaths, a rough music.

The trouble with the heaps was that they appealed strongly to the one ineradicable criminal habit of the Potteries: aggressive stone throwing. This was not so much an urban as a rural phenomenon. It was a form of localised xenophobia. On the moors, boys and young men would stone people from neighbouring villages, let alone total strangers. When the six towns were villages, they developed this habit into a military art, aggravated by commercial rivalry, and even after they became towns, the itch to ''eave half a brick at thee' remained. Wicked boys liked the stone heaps, which supplied them with ammunition in prodigious quantities. One morning I saw two grown-up men, faces contorted with terror, run for their lives near the heaps. At a distance followed two sweating, burly boys, with muscular, much-practised throwing arms, each with a heap of stones in his shirt, stopping every few paces and hurling a missile. They threw with accuracy, length and venom, and the rage on their faces indicated deep personal hatred of their targets. I was witnessing not some generalised xenophobia, but a family vendetta. The image of fear and fury remains in my mind to this day. Violence played so little part in our lives that its rare display was memorable.

When I was small, the heaps of stones were the limit of the territory I explored by myself. But with my sisters I went much further and these walks, punctuated by a picnic, were among the greatest delights of my childhood. Two routes in particular stand out. The first was the road to Knypersley Lake. There were two ways of beginning it. The first was to go down past the park wilderness, then turn left into the fields. This led into a sinister area of old clay pits, where men had dug for the raw material of the pots before the industry was organised on a large scale. These pits, shallow but sometimes with greasy water in them, were like photographs I had seen of the Western Front in the Great War, with its

The mineral railway, on the way to Knypersley Lake

deep shell holes. I liked this lunar landscape but the girls did not.

So we normally went another way. This led past the heaps of stones, down a sloping field and ended in a precipitous bank. At its bottom there was the little mineral railway and to the right lay Mrs Williams's whitewashed cottage, where the Master ruled. We would see her putting out her washing or feeding her chickens, and wave cheerily. However, we did not go past her cottage but turned left, along the line of rail itself. This was not as dangerous as it seems because the drivers of the little goods engines were all alone in the cabs, doing the coal stoking themselves, and relieved their boredom by sounding their whistles as often as possible. In any case we could hear the engines when they were still a long way off. Clare taught me to put my ear to the rails and listen to their high-pitched vibrations when a train was coming.

All the same, it surprised me, looking back nearly seventy

years, that so few restrictions were placed on people, children
included, going where they wanted in an industrial area
crowded with machinery of all kinds. Parents were expected
to warn their children of dangers and children in turn had to
heed warnings. As a result, there was almost limitless freedom
to wander. It is true you could not easily get past the porter's
lodge of a pot-bank because it was necessary to guard what
were enticingly called 'trade secrets'. But everything else was
open. This little railway was unfenced and it was fine to walk
on it. People said that if you put a halfpenny on a rail until a
train came, the engine would miraculously squash it into a
penny. But when we tried this the result was unsatisfactory —
the halfpenny certainly expanded but with a broken edge and
would not pass for a current coin of the realm of any
description. If an engine driver saw us he would sometimes
stop and have a chat: 'Art 'eading for Knapsey Lake, like? Oh
ar? Gives us'es regards ter t'fishes then. So long, ducks.'
('Ducks' was the standard Potteries term of friendly greeting.)

The rail line took us under a series of small bridges,
marking the road network of this Potteries fringe, where town
dwindled into open fields. The bridges were of dark-red
brick, made locally, but each was different. Unless money was
very scarce, the early industrial age always tried to beautify the
buildings it put up. Some bridges had little low-relief towers
on either side, with castellated tops, so that going under them
was like entering the main entrance of a medieval fortress.
Others had a hint of classicism: Doric or Ionic pilasters
guarding the hole and indentations above it. One bridge on
this insignificant little line even had a swirly hint of the
baroque, though such a word would have been quite unknown
to the mid-nineteenth-century builder-designers. There was
also a tunnel, curved and echoing, quite dark towards the
centre. We could climb up round it and go across the hill it

penetrated. But daring forced us to go through the ordeal, shouting and hearing the echoes to keep up our spirits, then listening for a train. Never once did a train come when we were actually in the tunnel, and even if it had there were recesses in the walls at intervals in which to shelter. But being in the tunnel had a tiny frisson of danger, which we relished.

When we emerged from the tunnel, we were in seemingly limitless green fields and woods, with patches of moorland. The air was fresh, the smuts had gone, the smoke clouds were low on the south-west horizon rather than overhead. But one giant monster lay in our path: the Chatterley-Whitfield mine. Coal had been mined hereabouts since the early Middle Ages, normally on a small scale from open-cast pits or shallow workings. Their detritus remained, overgrown for hundreds of years, often half a millennium. Later mines had been abandoned too, as we could see from holes going into shallow hills, stretches of rusted narrow-gauge rails, old iron wagons on their sides, all bearing the patina of time. Such places, in the quiet countryside, seemed to me even then full of romance and poetry. Or perhaps horror, I said to my sisters, if the skeletons of dead miners came out on dark nights to resume their labour, their bones rattling, the rusty coal trucks clanking. But Clare said that 'such superstitious nonsense' was an 'insult to nature', which had made the spot beautiful again – an old mine-working was an excellent place to find four-leaf clovers, possibly even gold coins – and Elfride thought that to harbour such thoughts was sinful. In any case, in daylight the workings were serene and spurs to historical thought of the kind I was already beginning to entertain: men in ruffs, wearing pouches and bright buttons on their shoes.

The Whitfield colliery, however, was a large going concern, full of activity and thrills. There was the main shaft, high and traditional, giant wheels spinning as the lifts went up and

down, disgorging groups of black-faced miners, clutching
their lamps and their empty bowls of Lobby, grinning and
laughing to be in the sweet air again. What particularly
fascinated and frightened me was a huge square basin where
the coal was washed, deep and dark, with water falling like
heavy showers from an array of pipes above. We could get
close enough to dip our hands into the turbid surface and
imagine the horrors of being cast into its depths. The noise
at times was infernal, for there was a formidable engine room,
emitting deep thump-thumps from its pumps and hissing
steam from its lifting gear. A man I liked called Mr
Hodgefield scrambled over the gears and pistons, sending in
jets of liquid from his oil can. He had a cheerful monkey face
and said, 'Is't thee, lad? Cum oop and see fer thiself!' But Clare
would not let me climb the iron ladder. In general, however,
she had a shrewd idea of what was perilous or not, and let me
wander freely and talk to the men. Mr Shirkley, the under-
manager, was a familiar figure to us. He told me, 'Ne'r look
down thi nose on coal, lad. It's the makking of England. T'ole
country's made of coal and so long as it last, England will ne'r
go 'ungry. Ee, but thee's a sensible kid, tha' knows that, dos
tha' not?' Alas, the giant wheels of Whitfield no longer spin
and miners, for better or for worse, no longer descend into the
earth's bowels. All is gone.

Beyond the pithead the real country began, half pasture,
half moor, and we descended into a delightful valley with a
meandering stream, the hills of Cowall and Biddulph Moors
rising to nearly a thousand feet on the other side. Just before
we got to Knypersley Lake there was a little dingle which
seemed to me then the most perfect spot on earth. The stream
bent round a jutting piece of grass and, emerging from this
peninsula (Clare had already instructed me in the elements of
geography) was a friendly tree, which stretched out over the

water. I say friendly because it was easy to climb and had a
perfect sitting place about eight feet up. There I would repose,
eating my sandwiches, high above the stream, watching the
crumbs float down to be snatched by the river fish bobbing up
to the surface. I liked to think that no one else knew of this
coign of vantage and it is true we never saw anyone at this
sacred spot. Clare could climb to the top of this tree and
sometimes did. More often, she scoured the wood around it,
looking for wildflowers, interesting insects, leaves, stones,
curious twigs, and evidence of the activities of birds and small
furry creatures. No picnic there went without some discovery:
a baby hedgehog, lost by its mother, the holes of water rats, a
hungry rabbit lured by a piece of cucumber, a wren's nest,
studied intently but left undisturbed, wild strawberries or a
handful of hazelnuts to chew. Elfride, by contrast, normally
had a book to read – Palgrave's *Golden Treasury*, Lamb's *Essays*,
Emily Brontë's *Poems* – or a notebook to fill with ideas for
stories or sonnets.

Then on to the lake, with trees all round its banks and a
magic well. There was usually a man there with a boat, angling
for the coarse fish that abounded in Knypersley. He was called
Mr Shuttershaw and said his family had always lived
thereabouts. I could tell from his accent that he was what my
mother called 'gentle-spoken', a Preston expression. So far as
I knew, he never did anything except fish and there was no
sign he ever caught any, but he kindly let us climb into his
boat and rowed us across. He said, 'Take ten very deep breaths
and expel all the Potteries smoke from your lungs. The air in
Knypersley Park is among the purest in England.' Under his
Ashanti hat, as he called it, his head was completely bald but
he had straggly tufts of grey-black hair over his ears. He said
he had lost his hair in the war, from shell-shock, and that only
fishing stopped his hands from shaking uncontrollably. He

kept sticks of raw or natural liquorice in his pockets, which
he chewed 'to stop myself from smoking, or I would puff
away all day'. He gave us a stick but we did not like it.

On the far side of the lake the country became wilder.
Foxes abounded and we saw one from time to time, taking
a lordly stroll through the grass and heather, to a stream, a
minute tributary of the majestic Trent. Clare spotted a
beaver's dam and made a drawing of it, and a diagram for her
Nature Book, which was crowded with drawings of leaves and
rare plants. When I was small, we rounded the lake and
headed for home. As I grew older, however, we ranged further
on the moor, sometimes walking three more miles to Rudyard
Lake, a much bigger and deeper mere. This was where Kipling's
father had courted his mother and proposed to her. But
Kipling never wrote a poem about the water which led to his
conception, or ever visited it. Clare wrote several, one about a
moorhen's nest she found on its shore, another about the wild
Norsemen who settled there. She also took up the theme of
the Saracens dwelling on Biddulph Moor. I wish I had these
poems now, to remind me of forgotten details – she was a
close student of nature's minutiae – but they have been swept
away in the slipstream of time.

The other favourite walk was to Mow Cop. This began with
Victoria Road, to the west of the park, where the rich Tunstall
elite, insofar as such a body existed, had their homes – large
detached villas from the Edwardian era. We speculated on
their interiors and imagined the luxuries they included.
Elfride wanted a library, a room containing nothing but books,
beautifully arranged in rational order, in fine, white-framed
bookshelves, with a roaring fire in the grate. Clare selected a
swimming pool, with a fountain at one end and a spring-
board. I wanted a studio with a high north light reaching to

the sky and a stove with a long funnel to the roof, such as I had seen in illustrations of bohemian studios in Paris. We all liked each other's ideas and concluded that a proper rich house should possess all three.

These dreams vanished as soon as Victoria Road ended and we climbed up a dreary thoroughfare called Pitt's Hill. Halfway up there was a track to the left, across another of those no-man's-lands in which the fringes of the Potteries abounded: patches of moorland, furze and gorse, odd cottages from wilder days, a farm or two, still lingering, abandoned coal- or clay-workings, the remains of an eighteenth-century furnace or grinding mill, and holes scooped out of the ground for some long-forgotten purpose. The landscape was crowded with the refuse of activities abandoned immediately they ceased to yield the meagre profits that had inspired them and the whole area bore the visage of eager youth decaying into old age before maturity had established itself.

The path lay upwards and culminated in a rocky outcrop, one of many which breaks through the skin of this part of England. Called Mow Cop and over 1,000 feet high, it dominates a wide area and is composed of Yovedale rock, a very ancient formation. In 1754 one Randal Wilbraham, owner of Rode Hall, built a ruined castle on the sharp summit as a landscape eye-catcher, which could be seen from his drawing-room windows. It was in essence just a tower and an arch, both crumbling fast when I knew it, and a flight of rocky steps leading up to them. But it made a perfect culmination of a picnic, especially for me.

For in the tower there was a round window, a 'bull's-eye', into which I could climb and sit, and eat my sandwiches and survey the whole of North Staffordshire and a great part of Cheshire – since Mow Cop is on the county boundary. This was a lordly seat. It inspired visions of grandeur: of knights

Mow Cop and its 'ruin'

moving in formation across the fields below, of siege towers being trundled up and trebuchets hurling giant stones or braziers of burning pitch and coals. The word 'folly' meant nothing to me and I could not imagine the motives of a man deliberately creating a ruin: to me, it had unquestionably been a genuine castle once, with real barons living in it and feasting in the tower where I sat eating deliciously soggy banana sandwiches. In fact, the only function Mow Cop had performed was to serve as a rallying point for gatherings of Primitive Methodists and to provide a headquarters during one of their hymn-loud camp meetings. Since the Primitives grew quiescent few had come there. In all our picnic visits I never saw a soul, so we came to regard it like the peninsula and its tree at Knypersley, almost as our private property.

Few people then had cars and if a place could not be reached by rail (and the network, though amazingly extensive, was not ubiquitous) it was not visited. Beyond Mow Cop a path ran through the woods and down the hill to the Macclesfield Canal. On the other side was what was then termed a gentleman's park, with woods and stream, formal gardens and fine trees, under which sheep and deer browsed. No one ever stopped us wandering through this park; in fact, we never saw a soul. Just outside its palings was the old house of the Mortons who made the park. It dated from about 1500, when houses were still moated, and was in the Cheshire style of black oak and white plaster. Nothing had been done to it since the time of the Armada. It had no electricity or gas, its walls leaned perilously and it had about it an air of delicious antiquity, untouched by time. We called it the Shakespeare House and sometimes the girls would read there, aloud, scenes from *Twelfth Night* or *As You Like It*. I can still hear Clare declaiming, 'If music be the food of love, play on. Give me excess of it.'

Me: 'What does excess mean?'

Elfride: 'More than you can eat.'

'How can you eat music?'

'It's a metaphor, silly.' I was used to this answer: the whole of life was crowded with metaphors, to make communication exciting but difficult. I liked to think of people chomping violins and taking huge bites out of drums.

We had no car. But we had bikes. When I acquired the huge freedom of movement provided by a schoolboy's (as opposed to a child's) bike, walking picnics were succeeded, as a rule, by biking picnics. That opened up for us a huge area of Cheshire and Derbyshire. It was easy to ride to Rudyard Lake by road and explore its wild far side. I discovered that it was not a natural lake at all but a stretch of low streamland, dammed in 1793 to provide copious water for the Trent and Mersey Canal, that arterial vein of Potteries industry. On the far side, despite its wilderness, there was a little railway, still working then, with stubby green engines pulling trucks of coal. The Romans had dug for copper there nearly two millennia before and there were caves showing plentiful signs of human activity long before that. My interest in history was already acute and omnivorous, and where knowledge failed, imagination supplied food for feverish speculation. I drew Roman soldiers guarding slaves who worked the mine and woad-painted men in skins emerging from their cavern homes.

There were outcrops like Mow Cop, some of impressive size: Congleton Edge, on the other side of Biddulph, and beyond it the culminating prow of the same ridge, a mountain called the Cloud. We could park our bikes by the side of the road running round its sharp north end, for no one stole bikes in those days, and climb up the precipitous slopes to find spectacular views to the north and west. From the Cloud, the Potteries appeared a vast smudge on the south-west horizon, a band of dirty grey and brown smoke, through which poked the tall chimneys and such landmarks as Father Ryan's great church tower and the clock tower of our park. There was a smaller outcrop called Hen Cloud, and a cluster which had been baptised by French prisoners of war who had been sent to hard labour in the Derbyshire mines. They called the outcrops *les roches* and the local tongue transformed the word into the Roaches — short for cockroaches according to my mother, who did not approve of rocky hills, destroyers alike of shoes and outer garments.

I also made bicycle trips with my friend Richard, son of our GP, Dr Halpin. He had a slightly weak ankle and a specialist had strongly recommended bicycling as a corrective. So Richard was keen and saw journeys by bike in terms of effort, distance and total mileage clocked up in a single day. His grand objective was to get to Chester and back, and when we achieved it he wanted to see 'how far we could get along the north Wales road'. I shared his enthusiasm for records, but only up to a point. I wanted to poke about old churches on the route, to explore Chester, which had encompassing walls, an ancient sandstone cathedral and a two-storey medieval shopping arcade, so sometimes I would go by myself. I explored the Potteries. I liked Longton, which seemed to me then the most romantic of the six towns, its dark pot-banks reflected in the water of the Trent and Mersey Canal, its gay barges, its almost perpetual fog spreading mystery through the dingy streets. I followed my father's habit of taking a sketchbook with me everywhere and drew some of the most shapely-looking kilns, including a conical one, which went back to the seventeenth century, or so I was told.

In those days, in the Potteries, there was always an un-employed man hanging around any point of interest, hoping to earn a penny and rich in information, true and false, if in no other commodity. Outside the house in Waterloo Road, between Burslem and Hanley, where Arnold Bennett had once lived, I paused to make a quick sketch. A lounging man immediately accosted me. 'Art drawing Mr Bennett's house, lad?' Then, after a pause, 'I knew Mr Bennett and his mother before 'im.'

'What was he like?' I asked politely.

''Ard. 'E was an 'ard man.' Rather like Hard Marshall, I reflected. Perhaps he should have been called Hard Bennett.

The man, who had a low, dirty cloth cap, a half-smoked cigarette tucked over one ear and a pristine one over the other, continued, 'As soon as 'e became a book-writer and earned good money,' 'e upped and went. They all do. 'E'd say, what's in Potteries for the likes of me? Nowt. So 'e goes to London and – what's it called? – Parees. Ar. 'E cum back at times, but 'ad nowt to say. And 'e 'ad that luke about 'im. As if ter say, Ah doan't know what tha' wants, but whatever it is, Ah'm not giving it thee. Ee, 'e was an 'ard man was Mr Bennett.'

At Trentham Park the Duke of Sutherland, who had got Sir Charles Barry to build him a palace, left in disgust in 1875 because of the smoke and pollution, and encroaching industry. He had married the richest woman in Britain, the hereditary Countess of Sutherland, and was made a duke as a reward. Long desolate and unkempt, the palace was pulled down in 1910, but the vast lake the Duke had created remained and his parterre, though it was unfashionable in the Thirties and badly kept up. What fascinated me was a tremendous mausoleum, just outside the palace gates. It was inspired by Piranesi, though I did not know it then. It seemed to me a work of terror and magic, and I drew it eagerly, although the problems of perspective it posed were beyond me.

As if on cue, a lounger appeared. 'Dost know what that is for, lad?'

'No.'

'Aye, well ah'll tell thee. It's to contain the dukes. Their dead bodies, like. Coffins. I dassay there's ten dead dukes in there.' Pause. Then, 'The duchess was t'richest liddy in England. 'Er would light ter fire with five-pun notes.'

'Do you believe that?'

'Noah. But 'er could 'ave dun if 'er ad wanted.'

I drew this well-informed man leaning against the mausoleum. That pleased him. It was a characteristic of the Potteries that grown-ups were always happy to talk to polite children. They treated me as an honorary grown-up, especially while I was sketching. I acquired a lot of local lore that way. Of course, much of what I was told was false or exaggerated. They knew the conical kiln was very old, so they said it was

The mausoleum in Trentham Park

'in Caesar's time'. Again, the mausoleum, I later discovered, was built about 1800, long before the dukes and contained none of them. My regard for chronological accuracy was already strong and I was developing a sharp nose for anachronisms. But I liked to listen to what loungers had to say. There was often, in their tangled mass of dubious information, a precious nugget of truth, which only they could convey. My mausoleum lounger told me that 'the Duke' had got Spode's or Copeland's, he wasn't sure which, to make a special set of bowls, in stoneware, but with his coats of arms on them, for his numerous dogs. He also said that 'the Duchess' had no inside handles for the doors of her carriage so she couldn't catch her dress on them, and anyway her footman opened the door from the outside. And the outside handle, he added, was made of 'pure gold' but 'bound on ter door by a special set o' steel pins, like, so ter street boys couldn't gerrit off'. I asked my mother about this fabulous duchess and was crisply told, 'She had the good sense never to live here.'

I often wondered, in retrospect, how my mother contrived to be so happy in a place she disliked, and which offered so few pleasures to her rich and vivacious, witty and gregarious nature. After all, unlike my father, she had no mission for which the Potteries provided an outlet. I think the answer is that she would have been happy anywhere, having a capacity for friendship which embraced virtually the entire human race. She made friends with all my father's assistants and many of his pupils. The nuns at St Dominic's, the brothers at St Joseph's were her devoted admirers. So were shopkeepers and tradesmen who called (except the greengrocer). A particular favourite was the man from Cantrell & Cockerell, the drinks people. He was called Mr Oakhanger, a tall saturnine fellow who looked a bit like my mother's favourite movie actor, Walter Pidgeon. It is a measure of his charm that he persuaded my mother to have a regular order of what he called 'them newfangled grapefruit crushes'. These delicious drinks, each in its individual bottle, were one of our few luxuries, served at dinner or high tea on special feast days. I thought this beverage infinitely superior to the popular children's drinks of the day, an apple juice called 'Tizer the Appetizer' and the great northern speciality, Dandelion and Burdock.

My mother had no time for gardening, which was left to Clare. And Clare's idea of a garden was a controlled wilderness, rich in wildflowers but with no formal borders at all, and with rare geological specimens ranged alongside hutches for tortoises, squirrels and hedgehogs. My mother said, 'Gardening is the last refuge of bored women.' But, as always, she had a song for it, which she taught me:

Mucking about the garden
Dear Old Uncle Joe.
Seeds begin to show.
Grass sprouts up to mow.
Mucking about the garden
Dear Old Uncle Joe.
Ripe tomatoes, apples and plums
Watching his onions grow.

'Of course,' my mother said, 'that's not *your* Uncle Joe.' He was her elder brother, a 'power in insurance' as she put it, rather implying that insurance was not something it was worth being a power in. She liked her brother Joe, 'when he's not being circumstantial' but I suspect had little time for Auntie Florrie, his harmless wife. However, her real dislike was reserved for the wife of her favourite brother, my Uncle Jimmy, handsome, dashing, clever and sophisticated. His union with Auntie Peg had been 'a wartime marriage'. 'She was very pretty *then*,' said my mother meaningfully. 'She got a job in a munitions factory and learned all the worst habits from vulgar girls. She even learned to *smoke*. Not a brain in her head. And now, look at her!' I thought Auntie Peg was a perfectly decent old soul, with a husky, cackling laugh, but my mother felt that Jimmy had 'married beneath him to put it at its mildest. It was a catastrophe and I know he regrets it, though of course he never says so.'

She also, I am sorry to say, disliked their son John, who often came to stay with us. 'That boy attracts dirt. He is a kind of *walking smut*.' She spent a lot of time scrubbing him. John, who had inherited his mother's brains, or lack of them, was in no way a bad boy. But he was foolish, accident prone and got into messes. He spent an entire day watching the operations of a municipal truck sent to repair a drain near our house. This involved pumping out the blockage, an accumulation of black rubbish, odiferous and stygian even by Potteries standards, then sluicing it with thousands of gallons of water pumped down under pressure. John offered to help and was eventually given a menial role, holding a piece of pump hose, by the grinning operatives. At tea that evening, having been scrubbed down, he announced, 'When I grow up, I'm going to be a-a-a-a *grid man*.'

My mother, a specialist in meaningful looks, gave a virtuoso performance, which made my father laugh uproariously. 'Oh, I expect you'll become a sea cook,' he said.

I had many cousins. The one I liked best was Elizabeth, youngest of three daughters of my mother's youngest brother, Uncle Wilf. He had been the baby she had looked after and as an adult she treated him as a comedy turn. 'Your Uncle Wilf has striven all his life for a first-class honours degree in pomposity and has finally achieved it.' This marked his promotion to become Director of Eastbourne Libraries, an important post since it gave him the right to control and censor the reading of all citizens of that salubrious resort. The idea of her little brother fighting a titanic battle to keep the works of D. H. Lawrence, James Joyce and Emile Zola out of Sussex-by-the-Sea filled my mother with mirth. 'He reads every book that comes in,' she said, 'and if he finds anything he deems an improper expression, out it goes.'

'What's an improper expression?'

'Anything your Uncle Wilf doesn't understand and thinks rude.'

'Like the Rude Lady?'

'Exactly.'

My mother's gardening song came from her childhood, as did most of her enormous repertoire. But in the Twenties and Thirties she discreetly added to it, though in theory she did not approve of jazz, swing, crooning or similar forms. She had a gift of learning by heart any song she liked after only one or two hearings. She loved Jerome Kern's superb lyrics:

> Now laughing friends deride
> Tears I cannot hide.
> So I smile and say
> When a lovely flame dies,
> Smoke gets in your eyes.

She taught me the words, at my request, of Shirley Temple's song 'Animal crackers in my soup', carefully explaining that when Shirley said she learned alphabet letters from A to Z, the Zed as we called it was pronounced 'Zee', to rhyme with 'me' on account of the vagaries of American pronunciation.

'Mummy, what does "stuff my tummy like a goop" mean?'

'It's an improper expression.' She also, when singing to me 'You made me love you (I didn't wanna do it)', explained that the 'wanna' was 'an American vulgarism' and the words 'want to' must be pronounced. She liked 'Carolina in the morning', 'The Camptown Races', 'If you knew Susie (like I know Susie)' and 'Ain't she sweet (coming down the street)'. She disapproved of Cole Porter, for obvious reasons, and Noël Coward 'because he has led on Gertrude Lawrence but never married her'. What she particularly liked were songs with a topical twist. Thus, when the Abdication Crisis finally broke, she delighted in singing:

> What's that coming down the street?
> Mrs Simpson's dainty feet.
> She's been married twice before
> Now she's knocking on Edward's door!

Next to singing my mother liked games: all games, with one

or two exceptions, and she was ingenious at inventing new ones. When I was little she played with me Snap, Pelmanism (the memory game) and rummy, for which she devised new and complex forms as I got older. She taught me draughts, dominoes and even chess, though the last she disliked. It was my father's favourite and he occasionally coaxed her into playing it, if he could get no other practice. But he would not, of course, allow her to talk. My only recollection of them having a dispute concerned chess. It was the terminal stages of a game.

FATHER (*impatiently*)   No need to ponder any further. You only have two possible moves, this – and that.

MOTHER   I have only your word for it. Supposing I think of a third.

FATHER   No, I have worked them all out. You have two moves only.

MOTHER   You are wrong. There is a third.

FATHER (*excitedly*)   I don't believe you – what is it?

MOTHER   This (*kicks table over and scatters pieces on the carpet.*)

That was the only time I heard my father swear in my mother's presence, for which he was instantly rebuked, my mother thus ending with the moral advantage too.

What my mother really liked was whist. She attended whist drives, which played the game in a variety of ways – military whist, for instance, with soldiers as tokens – and in which prizes were awarded. One reason she liked whist was that she was not forbidden to talk during the game. 'Games are for fun and fun means talk,' she said. She made many friends at the whist tables and they became part of her cast of characters whose doings she recounted to me. 'Mrs Slyman always revokes if she can get away with it. Well, with a name like that, what can you expect?' 'Mr Gorsybank always breathes heavily when he holds an unexpected trump.' 'Mrs Hooter is a bad loser. You can tell her father was an undertaker.' Mr Croxtonbank, who ran Tale's Pottery, had fingernails 'as black as pitch'. She said she was tempted to say to him what Charles Lamb said to Martin Burney: 'Martin, if dirt were trumps, what a hand you would hold!'

When her cousin Jack paid a visit and was not too pressed for time they played a mysterious game called Salford Rummy, invented in Manchester. It usually ended with Uncle Jack, who was one of my godfathers, giving me a sixpence. He was my mother's favourite cousin, albeit once or twice removed, a jovial, noisy gentleman, who roared 'Ho, ho' and 'That's my boy' and 'Tell that to the Marines' in reference to remarks of mine. He was, in those hard times, a commercial traveller, the area representative for a silver cleaner, mysteriously called Yar Ben. His competitor and desperate enemy was the salesman for another cleaning fluid called Town Talk. He told me alarming tales of this man's trickery, treachery and duplicity, and how he, Jack, thwarted his schemes. They ended, 'So that was one up for Jack, eh? Ho, ho! He wasn't born yesterday, was Jolly Jacky. Yar Ben for ever!' Sometimes my mother and he would sing a duet together from *No, no Nanette!* a 1924 hit, called 'Tea for Two':

> Picture you upon my knee
> Just tea for two, and two for tea
> Just me for you, and you for me ...
> Can't you see how happy we will be-ee!

It had two lines I particularly relished:

> Day will break and you will wake
> And start to bake a sugar cake!

It was my mother's belief that Uncle Jack had been hard-done by, had made a foolish marriage to a pretentious woman ('Your Aunt Cissie leaves a lot to be desired') and was too good for his job. 'Jack should have married a *superior woman*' (a favourite phrase of hers). My father was less charitable: 'An amiable fool!' I rather envied Jack his freedom to roam the county and frustrate the knavish tricks of Town Talk, and his unending jokes. 'Too many rings around Rosie,' he would sing, 'will never get Rosie a ring.' He told me, 'Remember, Paul, what the wise woman said:

> Laugh and the world laughs with you,
> Weep, and you weep alone.

Good advice my boy! Laugh while you can. There may not be jokes in the other place. It's a sad world and raising a smile is a good deed, eh, Annie? Ho, ho, ho, and away we go!'

My mother also loved quizzes of all kinds and they abounded on the new broadcasting service. I don't remember when we got our first wireless, though I recall the set itself vividly. My mother was afraid of it and of us listening to it. She laid down – perhaps she really believed – that listening to it was 'very expensive' and that my father's permission had to be secured before we could switch it on. This rule held until the war, though after she discovered 'radio quizzes' it was relaxed. At all our parties quiz games joined Consequences, Murder, Hangman, Telephone and the rest.

There was a marvellous addition around Christmas 1936 when I was just eight and still at St Dominic's. One of Elfride's school friends had been sent from New York a new game which had transfixed America. It was called Monopoly. Her set had New York street names, but an English version soon appeared with London streets. As there was absolutely no question of us being able to afford to buy such a game, Elfride sat down to make our own. Daddy supplied the appropriate boarding and material for cards. We soon had two sets: one with London street names, the second based on the Potteries, with Victoria Road, Queen's Avenue, Hartshill, Waterloo Road and even The Sytch. Clare drew a wonderful map for the centre of the board and we played this game relentlessly for the next year or so. Clare, alas, was not always available. She had won a scholarship and was studying geography at Manchester University under Professor H. J. Fleure.

Then came a new game. In the autumn of 1938 Elfride, who also won a scholarship, went to Oxford, where J. R. R. Tolkien was her professor. She was only seventeen and was then, I think, the youngest woman ever to attend the university. She came back that Christmas with a host of new ideas and among them was a desperately exciting card game, taught to her by a Chinese girl in her college. It was called Racing Demon and was fast, noisy, boisterous and exhilarating. We and our friends played it together, over and over again, sometimes when my father was in earshot. 'Ah,' he commented sardonically, 'our humble abode has, at last, been touched by Oxford civilisation.' (He was a Cambridge man.)

My mother, with all her love of games, was unattracted by these novelties. She thought Monopoly 'made young people greedy'. Racing Demon was to her an abomination, so different from the sedate tranquillity of whist and totally lacking its abundant opportunities for conversation. With Tom at work and wholly obsessed with his new possession, a Norton racing motorbike, and with both girls at university, our tightly meshed, intimate family was beginning to break up.

My mother and I grew closer together, conscious that,

before long, I would go away to school. She became my patient adviser and, if need be, loyal and indignant protector, through all the crises, minor in retrospect, overwhelming at times, which marked life at a fiercely competitive and strictly run boys' school. We read books together: Stevenson's *Kidnapped*, Keats's *Poems*, Tennyson's *Idylls* and, a favourite of hers, Hardy's *A Pair of Blue Eyes*. She continued to tell me her sagas and everything that was on her mind, and I continued to listen and sympathise, though much was beyond me. We loved the wireless, especially such programmes as *In Town Tonight*, which began dramatically with the announcer stopping the traffic in Piccadilly Circus, then interviewing famous people who were passing through London. We loved, too, Henry Hall and the BBC Dance Band. My mother said, 'You can tell he is a gentleman, unlike *most of those sort of people*.' By contrast, Roy Fox and Harry Roy and *their* bands were dismissed as 'fit only for nightclubs'. I am not sure on what precise evidence my mother made these absolute distinctions. She loved to divide the world into sheep and goats: her sheep were very, very white and her goats as black as pitch. She pronounced the word 'nightclub' with peculiar distaste and one of her poetic grimaces accompanied by dismissive body language. She had never set foot in one, I am quite sure, just as she had never, so she told me, visited a public house. As a result, by the time I went up to Oxford I was eager to go to nightclubs, though I now deplore them as much as she ever did.

We often visited the Ritz cinema, not so much in forbidden hours but when I came home from school (and sometimes we got up early the next morning to do my homework together). We saw moving and, to me, inspiring films about Rembrandt and Schubert, the second of which made my mother cry copiously. We saw *King Kong*, which she decided was 'tiresomely sentimental' – I thought it superb and still do – and Jimmy Cagney in gangster movies. She thought him 'ill-bred' and 'a bad example', an instance of her inability or unwillingness to distinguish between an actor and his part. She preferred Pat O'Brien because he always played virtuous police officers and because he 'came from the right part of Ireland'. She refused to see Greta Garbo at all because of some immoral behaviour in one of her movies. In general, she approved of Laurel and Hardy, at least for children, as they 'did nothing wicked'. But other comedy teams met with disquiet: Will Hay and his two subhuman assistants, the Three Stooges, whom she called 'brutal, unfunny and nauseating', and worst of all 'Old Mother Riley', in which husband and wife played a disgusting old woman and her daughter. My mother deemed this not only crude and unnatural but also, for some deep and obscure reason, anti-Catholic.

   She liked Claudette Colbert, Robert Taylor – up to a point: she said his legs were too short – and Clark Gable, the last pronounced 'a bit rough, and dreadfully American, but not wholly without charm'. She was quite shocked to be told a piece of information given to me by a knowing boy at school, that Gable had false teeth. 'Poor man, no wonder his pronunciation leaves much to be desired.' She loved Ronald Coleman and, still more, Leslie Howard. She deplored Charles Laughton because he was a lapsed Catholic, but nonetheless took me with her to see *The Private Life of Henry VIII*, regarded as quite shocking at the time. When Henry, before going into the bedroom of ugly Anne of Cleves, said, 'The things I do for England,' we both laughed without restraint, though she knew the joke was improper and I did not quite see the point. She put her hand in mine, as she always did when she was particularly happy.

＊

This period, insofar as I can disentangle my memories in proper order, was the last I spent in arcadia. I lived in what seems, in retrospect, a private Garden of Eden, but I became increasingly conscious that, even then, changes were taking place. One Saturday morning I heard the cheerful, impatient voice of Arthur Machin: 'Paul Bede! Paul Bede! Where is he?' When I appeared he said, 'Ahv summat to show thee, lad! Come with us.' (When Potteries people got excited, in those days, pronouns became exuberant too.) Outside our house, at long last, was *the van!* 'Gerra load o' that,' he said proudly, pointing to its smart white and green paint, and the announcement 'Jacob Machin & Son: High Quality Dairy Products'. He said, 'T' old man saw reason, not before time, and forked out. Ee, but it makes a grand difference. Well, lad, wot dust think, ay?'

'It's lovely, Arthur. It's a *beautiful* van.'

''Op in, then an' us'll go fer a spin.' So we did, and many times thereafter.

But even Arthur, sunny by nature, worried about what was to come. Everyone I knew did. There were hints even in the world of song. At this time my mother heard, liked and learned the words of an Irving Berlin song which, in retrospect, seemed prophetic. It was called 'Let's face the music and dance' – 'before the fiddles have fled and they asked us to pay the bill'. It ended:

> There may be teardrops to shed
> So while there's moonlight and music
> And love and romance
> Let's face the music and dance.

When she sang this I asked, 'What will the tears be for?'
She said, 'I don't know, but we live in a vale of tears.'

CHAPTER NINE

The Coming of
the Soldiers

TO ME THE 1930s were a prosperous decade because I was happy, and lived in a family where I was cherished and encouraged and, I fear, petted and loved more than was good for me and certainly beyond my deserts. But I began to realise, even at the time, that it was not so for grown-ups. I sensed they were anxious and that their fears were growing. One night about this time I lay in bed waiting for my mother to come and say goodnight. As was her custom, she brought with her a little oil lamp she put on my bedside table. It comforted me, I liked the warm oily smell, it was just enough to read by and, when I wanted to sleep, I could turn the little wheel by the globe and extinguish it. This time, however, as she came into the room, the lamp, held below her face, threw all the lines and wrinkles in it into sharp relief and I suddenly realised, with a fearful shock which still pains me today, that she was growing old. That familiar, infinitely beloved face had changed, unnoticed by me, and all her hard work and worries and responsibilities were beginning to show in it. Selfish and self-centred as I was, I was swept by a wave of tenderness for this patient, caring and hypersensitive woman, to whose heart I was so close and who was even closer to my own. I suddenly realised, and the thought came as a kind of relief, that some day not too far ahead, I would look after her as she had been looking after me. I asked her how she felt – a question I had never put before. She said, 'Oh, all right. As well as can be considering the crisis, and one thing and another.'

Crisis! This was a word which was heard ever more frequently during my childhood. It was Churchill who first made the word popular, when he published his war memoirs in the early 1920s. As Arthur Balfour observed about it at the time, 'Winston has published an enormous book about himself and called it *The World Crisis*.' Crisis had come back into everyday speech in 1931 with the financial troubles and from 1935 onwards it was never out of the headlines, first with the Abdication Crisis. Early in 1938 my sisters and I, getting a little tired of Monopoly even in our own Potteries version, began to devise a new, though comparable, game, more in tune with the times, we thought. It involved buying not streets but entire countries and building up empires of them to the point where competitors were exhausted by the time they had to pay, for landing on your squares. There was a map in the middle, with little cork stamps on each country, in which you planted your flag when you had bought it. It was called Crisis. You paid, not in stage money, but in soldiers.

I had been collecting soldiers since my fifth birthday, when I received a box of six, one of whom, in due course, became the first head of my army, under the name of General Ranter. He was a guardsman, in red coat and black trousers, and a bearskin. In the 1930s painted lead soldiers came in three basic categories. Standing soldiers, with static arms, were one penny. Soldiers with one moving arm, usually holding a rifle, were a penny-halfpenny. A soldier on a horse or a cavalryman was twopence. Cavalrymen who detached from their horses were an extra halfpenny. I am quoting Woolworths' prices but most other shops charged the same. These men were well modelled and painted, and good value. But they were brittle. During fighting, both in your own solitary games and in battles with soldiers belonging to other boys, heads were liable to snap off. A head could be mended, up to a point, by inserting a piece of matchstick into the head at one end and the body at the other. A soldier with a moving arm might lose it and it could then be put back, provided the little socket in the shoulder, or the ring at the end of the arm, was not broken. If either was, the arm was useless and had to be scrapped.

The third form of damage was when the two legs came apart from the stand. This was fatal. It is true that some boys had soldering sets and would heat the legs until they began to melt, and the stand too, then ram both together. The result, however, was always ultra-fragile and would break at the first touch of rough usage. After many attempts I concluded that it was not worth the effort and mess. Thereafter, soldiers without stands were retired from the army and kept in a special tin box of disembodied arms and heads, stands with nothing but feet attached, horses without riders – or legs in many cases – and bits of equipment, such as pistols, belts and hats, which had been detached from their owners and could not be restored. This gruesome collection was known as the Tin Hospital and was sometimes laid out for general inspection, though I never had more than two beds and one nurse, who soon lost her own head. I had an army doctor too but he broke his stand and became separated from his stethoscope, and so joined the cripples.

At one time my army numbered over two thousand bodies. It was divided into three main divisions. The first was the Red Army, consisting entirely of guardsmen in red jackets, plus Scotsmen in kilts or trews, provided their tops were red. General Ranter came from the Red Army and remained

Generalissimo (a name I picked up from General Chiang Kai-shek, the Chinese dictator) until he lost not only his head but his stand and went into the Tin Hospital. His successor, General Runner, also came from the Red Army, which of course was the senior branch of the service. He was so called because he was running with a right arm carrying his rifle. He lost this arm completely, but remained Generalissimo for a long time with only one arm, like General Raglan in the Crimean War, until he lost his stand. Then he too was retired, or 'Tinned', the term used in my army.

Then the view emerged that it was time for a change, so the third Generalissimo was chosen from the Brown Army. This category embraced all soldiers wearing khaki or nondescript uniforms ranging from German field-grey to Indian service sand colour. At that time khaki, which had been in use since the Boer War, still consisted of jacket, trousers and puttees, for battledress, though already 'in the works', had not reached the toyshops. The new commander, then, was a Great War figure. He was called, rather feebly, General Brown. But when I discovered that a recent Chief of the Imperial General Staff had been called Sir Archibald Montgomery-Massingberd, I decided that Brown was too undistinguished, so he was upgraded to General Buller-Brown, the name Buller featuring in a Boer War song my mother used to sing:

> Redvers Buller and Kitchener
> Roberts, Powell and Day,
> Forty thousand horses and foot
> Going to Table Bay.

Buller-Brown, though often criticised as old-fashioned because of his puttees, led the army with great distinction until literally crushed by Uncle Jack's boot, during field manoeuvres

— Uncle Jack being a keen follower of toy soldiery. He made ample amends by presenting the army with a military band, in red, something it had never possessed before, which he rightly said would 'cheer it up for its loss'. Buller-Brown's departure brought into play the third division, what I called the Mixed Army.

This consisted of all creatures on two legs and of comparable sizes, who did not fit into the two earlier categories. It was, in fact, a Foreign Legion. These men (and women) had been presented to me by relatives, guests and other benevolent ships that passed in the night, who did not always understand my requirements. They included a box of German Death's-head Hussars, French *poilus* and *legionnaires*, Afridi troops in red fezzes, various groups from the Indian army, mostly with turbans, Italian Bersaglieri, running, of course (they always marched 'at the double'), Spanish *Gardia Civil* and Australian diggers. There were some outstanding individuals: Dr Livingstone and Mr Stanley, Amy Johnson, the aviatrix, Sir Malcolm Campbell, who broke the world speed record in *Bluebird*, Captain Eyston, Helen Withers, the tennis ace, two versions of Don Bradman, the cricketer, Abraham Lincoln and George Washington (from a set of American presidents), John the Baptist and the film star Fay Wray, accompanied by her admirer King Kong, though he was too big to be fitted into most arrangements and anyway was made of plaster. There were also cowboys, Indians, Esquimaus, Zulus, Turks, Crusaders and Saracens. Buller-Brown's successor, the first Generalissimo chosen from the Mixed Army, was a ferocious Chinese pirate called Fang.

My army was rather comical, as this brief account suggests. All its officers had names and many of the other ranks too. There was some artillery, including a gun which fired silver-coloured shells. With my fretsaw I made a defensive system based upon the French Maginot Line, with circular gun turrets which rose out of the ground, in this case out of a cardboard box. The arrival of Dinky Toys made a difference, for though their tanks were out of scale with my men, I soon got accustomed to their incongruity. They were strong, finely modelled and realistic. In 1938, on my birthday, I was given the firm's military masterpiece, called 'The Mechanised Army'. It was a stroke of great generosity on my mother's part, not only because it was expensive but because it mirrored only too well the massive rearmament programme then taking place, which she dreaded as a portent of another world war. The long oblong box contained an impressive collection of modern vehicles, a heavy tank and a light tank, one of the new Bren-gun carriers, a two-ton lorry, towing a field gun and ammunition carrier, another towing an anti-aircraft gun, a scout car and staff car, and yet another lorry towing a field kitchen. I assigned a detachment from the Brown Army to this powerful unit, commanded by a one-armed veteran with a matchstick head called General Boot, because of his long shiny footwear.

I heard of wars and rumours of wars on the wireless, and there was endless political talk. The relationship between armies and their generals on the one hand, and governments and the politicians who composed them on the other, puzzled me. When my cousin John, on a visit, appeared in a splendid child's version of a general's uniform, I was impressed until he began to boss me around. Then I donned a king's outfit I had worn in a nativity play the Christmas before, and argued that a king came higher in the order of authority than a general and bossed *him* around. My mother upheld my version of constitutional theory but my father was more sceptical. 'Look at Mussolini and the King of Italy,' he said. 'And, more to the point, look at Franco.'

Franco, I knew, was called Generalissimo, like my Commander-in-Chief. And he appeared to be making himself ruler of Spain. I asked, 'What about the King of Spain?'

'He is in exile,' said my father sadly.

Spain, to him, was a personal tragedy. Of all the countries of the world it was, next to England, the dearest. He went there every summer if he possibly could, to draw its churches, cathedrals, monasteries and medieval buildings of all kinds, which in the early Thirties were still intact. He loved the simple people of Spain, whom he found invariably kind, honest and helpful. He said to me, 'The Spanish of all ages, both sexes and irrespective of their rank – from peasants to dukes – have a strong sense of honour, which gives them dignity and nobility. It is a great sadness to me that they cannot agree on how they should be governed.' He hated the Communists, 'controlled from Russia', and thought little of the Socialist government, 'feeble and undecided'. He was filled with horror at the attacks on the Church, which began while he was in the country drawing. Nearly 20,000 priests, nuns and monks were massacred, often with atrocious cruelty, and their convents and churches burned to the ground. Sacred objects of unsurpassed beauty and great antiquity were stolen, melted down for their gold and silver or simply cast into the flames in a frenzy of religious hatred. He could not under-stand how the Spanish, whom he loved, could do such things, any more than he could grasp the mesmeric power of Mussolini, whom he called a 'mountebank' (a word I immediately adopted and relished), over the Italians 'who understand art better than any other people'.

In his love of old Spain, my father was driven to support Franco who pledged himself to restore and respect it. But he disliked the man and his backers, especially the Nazis of Germany. So Spain to him was a tragic drama which could have no happy ending, and he daily followed events there with sighs and exclamations of 'Appalling', 'Outrageous' and, over and over again, 'Poor Spain, poor Spain!' He seemed to age, as the civil war harrowed the country he had delighted in, from east to west and north to south. 'I shall never go there again,' he said to me, 'I could not bear it.' I was once walking to church with him when a bedraggled left-wing procession passed us with a banner 'Arms to Spain!'. He sighed. 'Spain has enough arms already. Too many, alas.'

My mother kept her thoughts about Spain to herself. Whereas my father was a conservative in the sense that Edmund Burke was one, loving the past and anxious that its traditions should be adapted and changed slowly, rather than transformed, my mother was a Gladstonian liberal. She quoted the old campaign slogan 'Peace, Retrenchment and Reform'. She told me a story about her favourite uncle, Papa's eldest brother, my Great-Uncle James. As head of Pitman's in Manchester, he was a prominent figure in the city and lived in a substantial mansion in the Exchange division, which returned A. J. Balfour to Parliament. Balfour had resigned as prime minister at the end of 1905 and his Liberal successor, Sir Henry Campbell-Bannerman, held an immediate general election in January. She said, 'The weather was very bad. A lot of rain, even snow. I was staying at Uncle James's house. The doorbell rang and the parlourmaid came into the drawing room, where my uncle was listening to me play the piano. She said, "It is Mr Balfour, Sir, about the election." He rose and went to the door, and I followed at a discreet distance.

'Two tall men in top hats and with astrakhan fur-collared overcoats stood on the doorstep. When they saw Uncle James, they both lifted their hats. Mr Balfour said, "Mr Hynes, as on earlier occasions, I have come to solicit your suffrage, which you have been good enough to give me in the past. May I count on your support again?"

'Uncle James said, "I am sorry to say, Mr Balfour, that on this occasion it will not be possible."

'Mr Balfour nodded, said, "Good day, Mr Hynes," replaced his top hat, and he and his agent departed. I did not dare ask my uncle why he refused to do what Mr Balfour wished. But I heard later that the poor man lost his seat.'

My mother, of course, got her vote after the war and used it. She said, 'I never tell your father how I vote and he never asks, though he is dying to know. It's like the Confessional, a secret.' I never heard them discuss politics. That does not mean they did not do so. My mother could be counted upon to give a firm answer if any particular issue came up. She divided politicians into sheep and goats, even more strictly than she did other people. She had approved of Mr Asquith who 'should never have married that dreadful woman'. She added, 'He lost his eldest son in the war and never got over it.'

'Was that in consequence?'

'In consequence of what?'

'Of marrying that dreadful woman?'

'No, of course not, you imp.' Then, sighing, 'So many lost those they loved best and all for no reason at all. What good did it do? The Germans are at it again, and the Italians too, and the Japanese.'

'Mother, what was Lloyd George like? I wish I could draw him but he's too hard.'

'Too slippery, you mean. He told a lie upon his oath.'

'What was the lie about?'

'Never you mind.'

'Are all politicians bad, as Sir Oswald Mosley said on the wireless?'

'My Uncle James had a high opinion of Lord Derby. He

said he could always be relied upon to do the decent thing. He spoke with a Lancashire accent like the rest of us. We called him "the King of Lancashire".'

As it happened, Lord Derby's son, Oliver Stanley, was the first politician I actually saw – indeed, met. He was President of the Board of Education and as such came on a visit to St Dominic's. He was big, tall, fat, red-faced, genial and courteous. He shook hands, while doing his classroom tour, with Sister Angela and she introduced me as 'a bright young man'.

'Bright, is he?' said the Minister. 'Well, boy, date of the Battle of Hastings?'

'1066.'

'Right. Battle of Bannockburn?'

'1314'.

'Right. Battle of Agincourt?'

'1415'.

'God bless my soul, the boy's a marvel! Carry on, Sister, don't mind me.'

I knew these answers because of a mnemonic my mother had taught me, so there was no merit in my performance. But Sister Angela said, 'You did me proud.'

Politicians, then, were jovial, anxious to please and easily pleased themselves, to judge from my experience. As I grew older I got to know a few names from the wireless. Sometimes my father would ask me to repeat what I heard on the News. If I mentioned Major Attlee's name, my father laughed. 'No good will come of that nonentity' – he disapproved strongly of Labour's opposition to rearmament. Mr Chamberlain left him with mixed feelings, I gathered. He supported the Prime Minister, but felt him weak, indecisive and too innocent for the times. Chamberlain's Munich policy left him in despair. It also for the first time involved me in events. It was decided to issue the entire population with gas masks. Everybody had to collect them personally from the Town Hall. For reasons I have forgotten, there was nobody to go with me and I set out at teatime, aged nine, to collect mine. It was the height of the pre-Munich panic. Everyone expected war to break out within days, to be followed immediately by German bombing attacks on our cities. It was assumed gas would be used and that those without masks would die horribly. My father, who had actually experienced gas attacks on the Western Front, was

Queuing for gas masks at Tunstall Town Hall

sceptical. He thought the Germans would not use gas bombs and that, if they did, the attacks would harm few people, if any. But he thought it sensible we should all have masks, even though he argued they would provide no protection (he was right on all these points). So off I went.

Tunstall Town Hall was the target of a milling mass of people. I had never seen so many gathered together before. I had to struggle even to get into the Town Hall and then queue up the staircase to reach the room where the masks were handed out. The experience was frightening but also exciting. Some people were terrified. One fat woman near me fainted – the first time I had witnessed such an event. She had to be carried out. There were moans, groans, a great deal of swearing and endless pushing. The smell was indescribable. Some were drunk. I seemed to be the only child there. A woman pointed at me and addressed another woman next to her: 'Is 'im with thou?'

'Nay, 'ee doesn't belong to us.'

'Art alone then, lad?'

'Yes.'

'Ee, poor soul, push that lad up forward.' I became an object of solicitude to these kind women and was propelled by benevolent force, rather like a parcel, up the stairs and into the mask room. A grim man, with a tin hat on and a bristling black moustache, asked my name. I gave it. 'Address?'

'Park View, Queen's Avenue, Tunstall.'

He consulted a big black register, then looked at me narrowly. 'According to this, you don't exist. Prove you exist, boy.'

A belligerent woman, standing behind me, took up my cause. ''Ow can 'e do that?'

I was baffled. It was the first time I had been asked a philosophical question. I took refuge in the Catechism, most of which I now knew by heart. The first question in it was 'Who made you?'

That came closest to the grim man's question, so I answered, 'God made me, sir.'

The man was puzzled by the introduction of theology into the bureaucratic business of identification and hesitated. That lost him the argument.

The belligerent woman said, 'Aye, and God made thou and I, Mr Coalpie. So give the lad 'is mask.'

This cry was taken up by even more combative creatures behind me: 'Give 'im 'is mask, and doan keep us'n waiting.' A demotic noise broke out: ''And over mask, Jacob Coalpie'.

He took off his tin hat, scratched his thinning locks, put his hat on again, consulted the ledger, appeared to find fresh authorisation in it and said, 'Boy, I'm bending the rules in your favour. Gwendoline, fit this boy with a mask.'

So Gwendoline, a tall woman in a hairnet hat called a snood who made me put on a mask and breathe through it, said, 'That'll do thee' and folded it into a square cardboard box with string attached. 'There you are, duck,' she said, 'all prepared for modern warfare.'

I descended the Town Hall steps with the gas mask in its box, worn across my shoulder by the string. This piece of equipment became a permanent part of our lives, though most people mitigated the ugliness of the box, which in any event soon became greasy and squalid, by buying a gas-mask cover, manufactured in dark tartan patterns, or severe grey or black, or even in flaming colours, as is the fashion of the English, thus to prettify the ugly necessity. I was proud of my box though shaken by the struggle to obtain it. I was soon to be ten and it was a trophy of my growth into responsibility.

On my way home I paused, as was my custom, on the bridge over the Loop Line, and looked at the familiar view south into Burslem and the heart of the Potteries. Dusk was falling, and the flames of the kilns and furnaces were leaping. Glints of red and orange were reflected on the steel railway lines stretching into the growing darkness, on the slowly moving wheels of a shunting engine, pulling coal wagons up the slope, and on the rigid ladder of the signals. There was a sudden flash of white heat as the furnace door of the Fenton ironworks opened. I could just glimpse active, frantic figures silhouetted against the incandescence. As always, I felt the pulse of energy released, the excitement of vast power pouring out into the atmosphere. Huge volumes of smoke forced their way upwards into the sombre sky, their under-sides rosy and purple with reflected light. Sparks rocketed hundreds of feet, flames licked at the cloud masses. It was as though Burslem was a citadel under siege from relentless foes armed with great guns. The colours seemed to me exceptional that evening: indigo and madder, rose and a hectic red, which lit up chimneys and pot-banks, themselves belching blue and white flames as fresh quantities of coal slack were hurled into their greedy furnaces. The Potteries was putting on one of its best displays, the night of the gas mask.

After the panic days of Munich, however, life became hum-drum again. But I was more conscious than ever that changes were taking place. Hitherto, life had seemed immutably stable. The clock of history, as it were, had stopped. Both my parents were methodical people, who loved the past and its ways, though both were painfully aware that there were many things wrong with the world that ought to be put right. One day my father took me to see the Wedgwood works at Etruria. On the way, he pointed out to me old railway carriages, pushed into fields by the rail sidings, which were now used as houses by homeless people. I had noticed them before, scattered by the sides of the main line and the Loop Line and had assumed people had always lived like that. But he explained that it was a result of the poverty and unemployment brought about by the Slump, as everyone called it. Families lived free in these battered old coaches because they did not possess the six shillings a week to rent a terraced house. They had no heating or regular sanitation, no running water. But some had been painted. Others had window boxes of bright flowers. As our train passed, I waved and a woman, hanging out her washing, waved back. 'There aren't enough council houses for them,' my father said.

'Will the government build more?' I asked.

He shook his head. 'All the effort now is to build armament factories.' He added, 'People expect miracles from governments. But governments can do little to alleviate human misery. Often they make things worse. There was a wise old gentleman who came from Litchfield, not far away, who had our surname – Dr Johnson. He wrote,

> How small of all that human hearts endure,
> That part which laws or kings can cause or cure.

At Etruria, we looked at the Wedgwood works, the first major pottery to be built as a whole. 'Now,' said my father, 'I will show you a remarkable thing. You remember I told you that, because of mining tunnels close to the surface, our church had to be built on a huge concrete raft. Well, this building was put up in 1767 when they didn't understand such things. And mining went on after it was built. There was no concrete raft and the subsidence is terrible. You can almost see the building sinking.' He pointed to the road in front of the main block and the nearby canal. 'Look at those two. Once the road and the canal were level, so you could put the goods

The Wedgwood works at Etruria

from the carts straight on to the barges, for shipment to Manchester and Liverpool, and to the Grand Junction Canal to London. Now – you can see for yourself – the road has sunk below the level of the canal. It must be at least ten feet lower and still going down.' Indeed, from the canal towing path you could peer down at the people and carts using the road. I have since seen photographs, one taken in 1895 and one about the time my father took me to Etruria, which show strikingly, when compared, how fast the ground under the works was slipping.

'There are parts of the works,' my father said, 'which are fifty feet lower than when they were built. The buildings are very old and ripe to be modernised. Come along and I'll show you the oldest bits.' He pointed to a pot oven of a peculiar shape, still in use and puffing smoke furiously. 'See that? Built in the eighteenth century. It bakes China biscuit here. It ought to be replaced by a new electric furnace. But they daren't do it because of the subsidence.

'So, Little Paul,' he concluded, 'instead of rebuilding the works here, they are going to move the whole operation to Burlaston on the other side of Trentham Park. They are putting up an entire new works, on a virgin site, all electrified and surrounded by new model houses in which the potters will live. It's the beginning of the end for the Old Potteries. When you replace coal firing with electricity you don't need the bottle-shaped pot-banks. They'll all go in time and with them most of the smoke, and everything will look quite different.'

'And is that a good thing, Daddy?'

'Of course. And it's unavoidable. Pot-banks have to modernise. Otherwise, they go out of business. Wedgwood will do well with a new factory. They have some very good potters and designers.'

He took me round the showroom. 'Look at these new coffee pots and teapots. They call them Globes. They are designed by a genius called Norman Wilson, who is the manager of the works. Superb. This is a Bournvita jug and mug designed for Cadbury's. They have sold over a million of them. Beautiful, elegant, modern lines but no Picasso nonsense. Here's another fine coffee set designed by Keith Murray, a New Zealander, no harm in that. He's a good man too. This is a great age for design, Little Paul. Businessmen are at last beginning to recognise how important good design is. Look at this vase: it's called the Boat Race Vase. Designed by a brilliant artist called Eric Ravilious. There's a teaset designed by another clever young fellow, Rex Whistler. Here's a set with a garden implements design — Eric Ravilious again. And here's a piece of bad design: a coronation mug by an old friend, Laura Knight.'

'Why is it bad, Daddy?'

'Oh, it's ostentatious, fussy, gaudy, too elaborate. Simplicity and elegance is what you should aim at.' He smiled – and I have never forgotten that smile – 'Simplicity and elegance, like your mother.'

On our way back he reverted to my question. 'Change always brings losses. The Potteries is hideous, dirty, wasteful and, I suppose, inefficient these days. But it's beautiful. Your mother doesn't see it. Nor do most people. But I do and you do, Little Paul. The French have a word for it, as they do for most things involving art – *jolie laide*. The Potteries is an ugly woman who has a strange kind of beauty. I shall be sorry when they kill her off.'

We spent an increasing amount of time listening to the wireless in 1939. My father usually came home too late to hear the six o'clock news, but I had standing orders to report to him its main items. I became quite adept. I noticed again that any mention of Major Attlee (as he still was called) elicited a laugh and an ejaculation: 'That ass!' or 'That foolish fellow!' He, like my mother, dismissed Lloyd George completely – 'a fraud,' 'a Welsh windbag'.

But on Churchill my father was ambivalent. On this point he probably reflected majority opinion among men of his generation who had been through the war. To take the story forward beyond the limits of this book, I remember him saying, when the Blitzkrieg started early in May 1940, 'There's talk of sending for that adventurer Churchill.' Ten days later his mood had changed: 'We will have to turn to Winston.'

I am sorry he was no longer alive when, much later but when I was still a schoolboy, I met Churchill in the flesh on the steps of the Clifton Arms in Lytham. Mr Churchill gave me one of the giant matches he used to light his cigars. Thus emboldened, I said, 'Mr Churchill, Sir, to what do you attribute your success in life?'

He instantly replied, 'Conservation of energy. Never stand up when you can sit down. And never sit down when you can lie down.'

The prospects of peace were dealt a succession of heavy blows, which had an almost palpable effect on my father: Hitler's seizure of the rest of Czechoslovakia, Mussolini's invasion of Albania — savagely denounced by Father Ryan from the pulpit, not least because it took place on a Sunday — and dreadful news from the Far East, where Japanese bombing raids killed thousands of Chinese. A new magazine, *Picture Post*, which my father bought occasionally, published horrifying pictures of the corpses — the first dead bodies I had ever seen, even in photographs. (In those days it was considered improper to show dead white people, but yellow-skinned cadavers were allowed, just as it was permitted to show 'native' women bare to the waist, another source of alarm and fascination to me.)

One particular broadcast I recall with startling clarity: the announcement, direct from Rome, of the election of a successor to the dead Pope Pius XI. The Cardinal Chamberlain, we were told, had come on to the balcony of St Peter's. There, despite the crackling, we heard his voice: '*Habemus Papem ... Il cardinale Eugenio Pacelli!*' followed by an ecstatic roar from the crowd, acclaiming a Roman like themselves. My father said, 'He will have a pontificate of sorrow and strife.'

For me, 1939 was the coming of the soldiers. More and more men in uniform appeared on the streets, as Territorials and Reservists were called up. I still played with my soldiers and new names appeared: General McTrusty Steel, commander of the Tank Army, a new formation. He was called McTrusty because, incongruously, he wore a kilt, though his replacement head, on a matchstick, was that of a German storm-trooper in coal-scuttle helmet, hence his surname Steel.

But my interest was shifting to the navy, thanks to my fretsaw and a marvellous present from Uncle Jack of an old volume of *Jane's Fighting Ships*, the authoritative inventory of the world's navies, complete with hundreds of photographs and plans. I started to make elaborate scale models of battleships in wood, with masts and guns of pins, with their heads cut off by pliers. They were painted dark-grey, and their names, tonnages and other salient facts painted on their flat bottoms in white. They were much admired and my output was steady. Hence, as toy factories were already turning over to armaments and toys were thus in short supply, my father took me to Huntbach's, with samples to show. He was a natural salesman and experienced in pleading for jobs for his students. So he made a deal and I earned my first regular money by making warships. Huntbach's demanded regular invoices, however, so I designed some and my father had them lithographed: my firm was called Ponkatoys, following a suggestion by my sister Elfride. I still, somewhere, have one of these sheets.

War against the Nazis followed with a kind of tragic inevitability. My mother, father and I all listened to the fatal broadcast at 11 a.m. on the morning of Sunday 3 September. To this day I can remember almost every word Neville Chamberlain spoke, especially, 'No such reply [to our ultimatum] has been received. In consequence, we are now at war with Germany. It is an evil thing that we are fighting.' I did not express but hid in my heart a feeling of exultation, that history had not ended after all, that great events were impending which I would witness, and that an age of heroism and excitement had opened. Then I looked up and saw my father's face and written on it were the lines of deep despair, the greyness of hopes dashed for ever, of pain recalled and suffering to be endured again. I had been uneasily aware that he was ageing, his breathing becoming more difficult, his eyes deeper set, his hair thinning fast. Now he seemed to have grown suddenly much older and I saw the shadow of the growing exhaustion that would end his life three years later. A casualty of the First World War, he would be a victim of the second, killed by overwork, shortages of staff and sheer worry.

He put his head in his hands for a long time after Chamberlain had ceased speaking. I was subdued and quiet, matching his mood, though by the evening I had already launched into my own war effort: a handwritten and drawn single-copy magazine about the conflict, brazenly called 'Facts', with profuse illustrations of the latest weapons.

My mother said little about the war that day, but was unusually watchful and anxious. The next day, Monday, her worst suspicions were confirmed. My brother Tom returned triumphant and announced, 'I have enlisted in the army as a volunteer for the duration. They have accepted me in the Hussars. I am in the HEAVY TANKS.' My mother's face reminded me of paintings of the Madonna weeping at the foot of the cross. She did not weep. She was, rather, a study in resigned misery. She remembered the day, a quarter century before, when all six of the young men closest to her had similarly enlisted – to return, if they returned at all – changed, hurt and much older. She bore the blow bravely, but she clutched me closer to her side.

I was nearly eleven and it was, I suppose, the end of my childhood. Indeed, it was the end of our family as I had known it. My brother went to the war and returned, six years later, his health ruined. My sisters took degrees and moved away to work in distant places. I went to boarding school. After my father died my mother left the Potteries, never to return.

When I visited the place, nearly half a century later, all had changed. The smoke, the soot, the smog and fog had gone. The coal mines were still. The railways, except for one main line, had vanished. There seemed no heavy industrial activity at all. I saw no slums either. Most of all, a thousand bottle-shaped pot-banks, the main and essential ingredient of that unique landscape, had been demolished. One or two survivors formed an 'industrial museum'. Every element of dreary and uniform modernity had been introduced. It looked like any-where else in England. It was clean, comparatively prosperous, comfortable after a fashion and totally without character. The *jolie laide* had had a drastic facelift and was no doubt a happier creature in consequence. But in the process she had lost her strange, romantic beauty; and, I suspect, her soul.

1	2	3	4	5	6	7	8	9	10	11	12	13	14	15
16	17	18	19	20	21	22	23	24	25	26	27	28	29	30
31	32	33	34	35	36	37	38	39	40	41	42	43	44	45
46	47	48	49	50	51	52	53	54	55	56	57	58	59	60
61	62	63	64	65	66	67	68	69	70	71	72	73	74	75
76	77	78	79	80	81	82	83	84	85	86	87	88	89	90
91	92	93	94	95	96	97	98	99	100					

101	102	103	104	105	106	107	108	109	110	111	112	113	114	115
116	117	118	119	120	121	122	123	124	125	126	127	128	129	130
131	132	133	134	135	136	137	138	139	140	141	142	143	144	145
146	147	148	149	150	151	152	153	154	155	156	157	158	159	160
161	162	163	164	165	166	167	168	169	170	171	172	173	174	175
176	177	178	179	180	181	182	183	184	185	186	187	188	189	190
191	192	193	194	195	196	197	198	199	200					

201	202	203	204	205	206	207	208	209	210	211	212	213	214	215
216	217	218	219	220	221	222	223	224	225	226	227	228	229	230
231	232	233	234	235	236	237	238	239	240	241	242	243	244	245
246	247	248	249	250	251	252	253	254	255	256	257	258	259	260
261	262	263	264	265	266	267	268	269	270	271	272	273	274	275
276	277	278	279	280	281	282	283	284	285	286	287	288	289	290
291	292	293	294	295	296	297	298	299	300					

301	302	303	304	305	306	307	308	309	310	311	312	313	314	315
316	317	318	319	320	321	322	323	324	325	326	327	328	329	330
331	332	333	334	335	336	337	338	339	340	341	342	343	344	345
346	347	348	349	350	351	352	353	354	355	356	357	358	359	360
361	362	363	364	365	366	367	368	369	370	371	372	373	374	375
376	377	378	379	380	381	382	383	384	385	386	387	388	389	390
391	392	393	394	395	396	397	398	399	400					

401	402	403	404	405	406	407	408	409	410	411	412	413	414	415
416	417	418	419	420	421	422	423	424	425	426	427	428	429	430
431	432	433	434	435	436	437	438	439	440	441	442	443	444	445
446	447	448	449	450	451	452	453	454	455	456	457	458	459	460
461	462	463	464	465	466	467	468	469	470	471	472	473	474	475
476	477	478	479	480	481	482	483	484	485	486	487	488	489	490
491	492	493	494	495	496	497	498	499	500					

M/c 3209

M/c 3318

M/c 3318A